READING IN THE CONTENT AREAS

LITERATURE 2

Laura Stark Johnson

PERMISSIONS

ISBN 0-88336-112-4

©1990

 New Readers Press
Publishing Division of Laubach Literacy
1320 Jamesville Ave., Syracuse, New York 13210

Printed in the United States of America

Project Editor: Christina M. Jagger
Manuscript Editor: Margaret Duckett
Cover Design: Patricia Rapple
Cover Art: Stephen Rhodes
Composition: Anne Hyde

9 8

Table of Contents

Unit 1: Short Stories

A story to me means a plot where there is some surprise...
Because that is how life is—full of surprises.
                                                    Issac Bashevis Singer

The world is full of stories. From ancient times to the present, stories have been a popular form of entertainment. Stories also provide insight into why people behave as they do. In one story in this unit, you'll discover why a person risks his life for another. In another story, you'll observe how a man finds the strength to endure hardship. In a third story, you'll learn how a young boy seeks to fulfill one basic need that all human beings share.

In order to understand people's behavior better, it helps to examine the conflicts they face. A conflict is a struggle between opposing forces. The conflict may be external, a struggle with another person or against Nature. Or there may be an internal conflict, a struggle inside the person, with his or her own personality. Identifying the conflict in a short story will reveal why characters decide on certain courses of action.

In addition to characters who face a conflict, short stories contain the elements of setting, plot and theme. The setting is the time and place in which the story's action occurs. The action, or series of events, is called the plot. Early in the plot, suspense is aroused. You'll want to find out what happens next. The theme is the main topic of each short story. Because you bring your own experiences and thoughts to a story, your understanding of the theme is often personal.

The elements of conflict, character, setting, plot, and theme can combine to produce literature that will stimulate the minds and emotions of readers for years to come.

What would you do if a friend gave up on life? In this short story, Sue and Johnsy share a studio apartment in New York City. Johnsy develops pneumonia and grows weaker day by day. Her roommate and Mr. Behrman, the neighbor downstairs, are alarmed that Johnsy has lost her will to live. Read to find out the powerful influence the mind has on the body.

The Last Leaf

O. Henry (1862–1910)

In a little district west of Washington Square the streets have run crazy and broken themselves into small strips called "places." These "places" make strange angles and curves. One street crosses itself a time or two. An artist once discovered a valuable possibility in this street. Suppose a collector with a bill for paints, paper and canvas should, in traversing this route, suddenly meet himself coming back, without a cent having been paid on account!

So, to quaint old Greenwich Village the art people soon came prowling, hunting for north windows and eighteenth-century gables and Dutch attics and low rents. Then they imported some pewter mugs and a chafing dish or two from Sixth Avenue, and became a "colony."

At the top of a squatty, three-story brick Sue and Johnsy had their studio. "Johnsy" was familiar for Joanna. One was from Maine; the other from California. They had met at the *table d'hôte*[1] of an Eighth Street "Delmonico's," and found their tastes in art, chicory salad and bishop sleeves so congenial that the joint studio resulted.

That was in May. In November a cold, unseen stranger, whom the doctors called Pneumonia, stalked

---

1. *table d'hôte*: complete meal offered at one price.

about the colony, touching one here and there with his icy fingers. Over on the east side this ravager strode boldly, smiting his victims by scores, but his feet trod slowly through the maze of the narrow and moss-grown "places."

Mr. Pneumonia was not what you would call a chivalric old gentleman. A mite of a little woman with blood thinned by California zephyrs was hardly fair game for the red-fisted, short-breathed old duffer. But Johnsy he smote; and she lay, scarcely moving, on her painted iron bedstead, looking through the small Dutch window-panes at the blank side of the next brick house.

One morning the busy doctor invited Sue into the hallway with a shaggy, gray eyebrow.

"She has one chance in—let us say, ten," he said, as he shook down the mercury in his clinical thermometer. "And that chance is for her to want to live. This way people have of lining-up on the side of the undertaker makes the entire pharmacopoeia look silly. Your little lady has made up her mind that she's not going to get well. Has she anything on her mind?"

"She—she wanted to paint the Bay of Naples some day," said Sue.

"Paint?—bosh! Has she anything on her mind worth thinking about twice—a man for instance?"

"A man?" said Sue, with a jew's-harp twang in her voice. "Is a man worth—but, no, doctor; there is nothing of the kind."

"Well, it is the weakness, then," said the doctor. "I will do all that science, so far as it may filter through my efforts, can accomplish. But whenever my patient begins to count the carriages in her funeral procession I subtract 50 percent from the curative powers of medicines. If you will get her to ask one question about the new winter styles in cloak sleeves I will promise you a one-in-five chance for her, instead of one in ten."

After the doctor had gone Sue went into the workroom and cried a Japanese napkin to a pulp. Then she swaggered into Johnsy's room with her drawing board, whistling ragtime.

Johnsy lay, scarcely making a ripple under the bedclothes, with her face toward the window. Sue stopped whistling, thinking she was asleep.

She arranged her board and began a pen-and-ink drawing to illustrate a magazine story. Young artists must pave their way to Art by drawing pictures for magazine stories that young authors write to pave their way to Literature.

As Sue was sketching a pair of elegant horseshow riding trousers and a monocle on the figure of the hero, an Idaho cowboy, she heard a low sound, several times repeated. She went quickly to the bedside.

Johnsy's eyes were open wide. She was looking out the window and counting—counting backward.

"Twelve," she said, and a little later "eleven"; and then "ten," and "nine"; and then "eight" and "seven," almost together.

Sue looked solicitously out of the window. What was there to count? There was only a bare, dreary yard to be seen, and the blank side of the brick house twenty feet away. An old, old ivy vine, gnarled and decayed at the roots, climbed halfway up the brick wall. The cold breath of autumn had stricken its leaves from the vine until its skeleton branches clung, almost bare, to the crumbling bricks.

"What is it, dear?" asked Sue.

"Six," said Johnsy, in almost a whisper. "They're falling faster now. Three days ago there were almost a hundred. It made my head ache to count them. But now it's easy. There goes another one. There are only five left now."

"Five what, dear? Tell your Sudie."

"Leaves. On the ivy vine. When the last one falls I must go, too. I've known that for three days. Didn't the doctor tell you?"

"Oh, I never heard of such nonsense," complained Sue, with magnificent scorn. "What have old ivy leaves to do with your getting well? And you used to love that vine so, you naughty girl. Don't be a goosey. Why, the doctor told me this morning that your chances for getting well real soon were—let's see exactly what he said—he said the chances were ten to one! Why, that's almost as good a chance as we have in New York when we ride on the street cars or walk past a new building. Try to take some broth now, and let Sudie go back to her drawing, so she can sell the editor man with it, and buy port wine for her sick child, and pork chops for her greedy self."

"You needn't get any more wine," said Johnsy, keeping her eyes fixed out the window. "There goes another. No, I don't want any broth. That leaves just four. I want to see the last one fall before it gets dark. Then I'll go, too."

"Johnsy, dear," said Sue, bending over her, "will you promise me to keep your eyes closed, and not look out the window until I am done working? I must hand those drawings in by tomorrow. I need the light, or I would draw the shade down."

"Couldn't you draw in the other room?" asked Johnsy, coldly.

"I'd rather be here by you," said Sue. "Besides, I don't want you to keep looking at those silly ivy leaves."

"Tell me as soon as you have finished," said Johnsy, closing her eyes, and lying white and still as a fallen statue, "because I want to see the last one fall. I'm tired of waiting. I'm tired of thinking. I want to turn loose my hold on everything, and go sailing down, down, just like one of those poor, tired leaves."

"Try to sleep," said Sue. "I must call Behrman up to be my model for the old hermit miner. I'll not be gone a minute. Don't try to move 'til I come back."

Old Behrman was a painter who lived on the ground floor beneath them. He was past sixty and had a Michael Angelo's Moses beard curling down from the head of a satyr along the body of an imp. Behrman was a failure in art. Forty years he had wielded the brush without getting near enough to touch the hem of his Mistress's robe. He had been always about to paint a masterpiece, but had never yet begun it. For several years he had painted nothing except now and then a daub in the line of commerce or advertising. He earned a little by serving as a model to those young artists in the colony who could not pay the price of a professional. He drank gin to excess, and still talked of his coming masterpiece. For the rest he was a fierce little old man, who scoffed terribly at softness in any one, and who regarded himself as especial mastiff-in-waiting[2] to protect the two young artists in the studio above.

Sue found Behrman smelling strongly of juniper berries in his dimly lighted den below. In one corner was a blank canvas on an easel that had been waiting there for twenty-five years to receive the first line of the masterpiece. She told him of Johnsy's fancy, and how she feared she would, indeed, light and fragile as a leaf herself, float away, when her slight hold upon the world grew weaker.

Old Behrman, with his red eyes plainly streaming, shouted his contempt and derision for such idiotic imaginings.

"Vass!" he cried. "Is dere people in de world mit der foolishness to die because leafs dey drop off from a confounded vine? I haf not heard of such a thing. No, I will not bose as a model for your fool hermit-dunderhead. Vy do you allow dot silly

---

2. **mastiff-in-waiting:** watchdog.

pusiness to come in der brain of her? Ach, dot poor leetle Miss Yohnsy."

"She is very ill and weak," said Sue, "and the fever has left her mind morbid and full of strange fancies. Very well, Mr. Behrman, if you do not care to pose for me, you needn't. But I think you are a horrid old—old flibbertigibbet."

"You are just like a woman!" yelled Behrman. "Who said I will not bose? Go on. I come mit you. For half an hour I haf peen trying to say dot I am ready to bose. Gott! dis is not any blace in which one so goot as Miss Yohnsy shall lie sick. Some day I vill baint a masterpiece, and ve shall all go away. Gott! yes."

Johnsy was sleeping when they went upstairs. Sue pulled the shade down to the windowsill, and motioned Behrman into the other room. In there they peered out the window fearfully at the ivy vine. Then they looked at each other for a moment without speaking. A persistent, cold rain was falling, mingled with snow. Behrman, in his old blue shirt, took his seat as the hermit miner on an upturned kettle for a rock.

When Sue awoke from an hour's sleep the next morning she found Johnsy with dull, wide-open eyes staring at the drawn green shade.

"Pull it up; I want to see," she ordered, in a whisper.

Wearily Sue obeyed.

But, lo! after the beating rain and fierce gusts of wind that had endured through the livelong night, there yet stood out against the brick wall one ivy leaf. It was the last on the vine. Still dark green near its stem, but with its serrated edges tinted with the yellow of dissolution and decay, it hung bravely from a branch some twenty feet above the ground.

"It is the last one," said Johnsy. "I thought it would surely fall during the night. I heard the wind. It will fall today, and I shall die at the same time."

"Dear, dear!" said Sue, leaning her worn face down to the pillow, "think of me, if you won't think of yourself. What would I do?"

But Johnsy did not answer. The lonesomest thing in all the world is a soul when it is making ready to go on its mysterious, far journey. The fancy seemed to possess her more strongly as one by one the ties that bound her to friendship and to earth were loosed.

The day wore away, and even through the twilight they could see the lone ivy leaf clinging to its stem against the wall. And then, with the coming of the night the north wind was again loosed, while the rain still beat against the windows and pattered down from the low Dutch eaves.

When it was light enough Johnsy, the merciless, commanded that the shade be raised.

The ivy leaf was still there.

Johnsy lay for a long time looking at it. And then she called to Sue, who was stirring her chicken broth over the gas stove.

"I've been a bad girl, Sudie," said Johnsy. "Something has made that last leaf stay there to show me how wicked I was. It is a sin to want to die.

You may bring me a little broth now, and some milk with a little port in it, and—no; bring me a hand-mirror first, and then pack some pillows about me, and I will sit up and watch you cook."

An hour later she said:

"Sudie, some day I hope to paint the Bay of Naples."

The doctor came in the afternoon, and Sue had an excuse to go into the hallway as he left.

"Even chances," said the doctor, taking Sue's thin, shaking hand in his. "With good nursing you'll win. And now I must see another case I have downstairs. Behrman, his name is—some kind of an artist, I believe. Pneumonia, too. He is an old, weak man, and the attack is acute. There is no hope for him; but he goes to the hospital today to be made more comfortable."

The next day the doctor said to Sue: "She's out of danger. You've won. Nutrition and care now—that's all."

And that afternoon Sue came to the bed where Johnsy lay, contentedly knitting a very blue and very useless woollen shoulder scarf, and put one arm around her, pillows and all.

"I have something to tell you, white mouse," she said. "Mr. Behrman died of pneumonia today in the hospital. He was ill only two days. The janitor found him on the morning of the first day in his room downstairs helpless with pain. His shoes and clothing were wet through and icy cold. They couldn't imagine where he had been on such a dreadful night. And then they found a lantern, still lighted, and a ladder that had been dragged from its place, and some scattered brushes, and a palette with green and yellow colors mixed on it, and—look out the window, dear, at the last ivy leaf on the wall. Didn't you wonder why it never fluttered or moved when the wind blew? Ah, darling, it's Behrman's masterpiece—he painted it there the night that the last leaf fell."

Have you ever heard of a "catbird seat"? Someone in the catbird seat has it as good as "a batter with three balls and no strikes on him." The catbird seat is a favorable position to be in. Read and enjoy this short story about someone who sat in the catbird seat once too often.

The Catbird Seat

James Thurber (1894–1961)

Mr. Martin bought the pack of Camels on Monday night in the most crowded cigar store on Broadway. It was theatre time and seven or eight men were buying cigarettes. The clerk didn't even glance at Mr. Martin, who put the pack in his overcoat pocket and went out. If any of the staff at F & S had seen him buy the cigarettes, they would have been astonished, for it was generally known that Mr. Martin did not smoke, and never had. No one saw him.

It was just a week to the day since Mr. Martin had decided to rub out Mrs. Ulgine Barrows. The term "rub out" pleased him because it suggested nothing more than the correction of an error—in this case an error of Mr. Fitweiler. Mr. Martin had spent each night of the past week working out his plan and examining it. As he walked home now he went over it again. For the hundredth time he resented the element of imprecision, the margin of guesswork that entered into the business. The project as he had worked it out was casual and bold, the risks were considerable. Something might go wrong anywhere along the line. And therein lay the cunning of his scheme. No one would ever see in it the cautious, painstaking hand of Erwin Martin, head of the filing department at F & S, of whom Mr. Fitweiler had once said, "Man is fallible[1] but Martin

---

1. **fallible**: capable of making mistakes.

isn't." No one would see his hand, that is, unless it were caught in the act.

Sitting in his apartment, drinking a glass of milk, Mr. Martin reviewed his case against Mrs. Ulgine Barrows, as he had every night for seven nights. He began at the beginning. Her quacking voice and braying laugh had first profaned the halls of F & S on March 7, 1941 (Mr. Martin had a head for dates). Old Roberts, the personnel chief, had introduced her as the newly appointed special adviser to the president of the firm, Mr. Fitweiler. The woman had appalled Mr. Martin instantly, but he hadn't shown it. He had given her his dry hand, a look of studious concentration, and a faint smile. "Well," she had said, looking at the papers on his desk, "are you lifting the oxcart out of the ditch?" As Mr. Martin recalled that moment, over his milk, he squirmed slightly. He must keep his mind on her crimes as a special adviser, not on her peccadillos as a personality. This he found difficult to do, in spite of entering an objection and sustaining it. The faults of the woman as a woman kept chattering on in his mind like an unruly witness. She had, for almost two years now, baited him. In the halls, in the elevator, even in his own office, into which she romped now and then like a circus horse, she was constantly shouting these silly little questions at him. "Are you lifting the oxcart out of the ditch? Are you tearing up the pea patch? Are you hollering down the rain barrel? Are you scraping around the bottom of the pickle barrel? Are you sitting in the catbird seat?"

"Are you lifting the oxcart out of the ditch?"

It was Joey Hart, one of Mr. Martin's two assistants, who had explained what the gibberish meant. "She must be a Dodger fan," he had said. "Red Barber announces the Dodger games over the radio and he uses those expressions—picked 'em up down South." Joey had gone on to explain one or two. "Tearing up the pea patch" meant going on a rampage; "sitting in the catbird seat" meant sitting pretty, like a batter with three balls and no strikes on him. Mr. Martin dismissed all this with an effort. It had been annoying, it had driven him near to distraction, but he was too solid a man to be moved to murder by anything so childish. It was fortunate, he reflected as he passed on to the important charges against Mrs.

Barrows, that he had stood up under it so well. He had maintained always an outward appearance of polite tolerance. "Why, I even believe you like the woman," Miss Paird, his other assistant, had once said to him. He had simply smiled.

A gavel rapped in Mr. Martin's mind and the case proper was resumed. Mrs. Ulgine Barrows stood charged with willful, blatant, and persistent attempts to destroy the efficiency and system of F & S. It was competent, material, and relevant to review her advent and rise to power. Mr. Martin had got the story from Miss Paird, who seemed always able to find things out. According to her, Mrs. Barrows had met Mr. Fitweiler at a party, where she had rescued him from the embraces of a powerfully built drunken man who had mistaken the president of F & S for a famous retired Middle Western football coach. She had led him to a sofa and somehow worked upon him a monstrous magic. The aging gentleman had jumped to the conclusion there and then that this was a woman of singular attainments, equipped to bring out the best in him and in the firm. A week later he had introduced her into F & S as his special adviser. On that day confusion got its foot in the door. After Miss Tyson, Mr. Brundage, and Mr. Bartlett had been fired and Mr. Munson had taken his hat and stalked out, mailing in his resignation later, old Roberts had been emboldened to speak to Mr. Fitweiler. He mentioned that Mr. Munson's department had been "a little disrupted" and hadn't they perhaps better resume the old system there? Mr. Fitweiler had said certainly not. He had the greatest faith in Mrs. Barrows' ideas. "They require a little seasoning, a little seasoning, is all," he had added. Mr. Roberts had given it up. Mr. Martin reviewed in detail all the changes wrought by Mrs. Barrows. She had begun chipping at the cornices of the firm's edifice and now she was swinging at the foundation stones with a pickaxe.

Mr. Martin came now, in his summing up, to the afternoon of Monday, November 2, 1942—just one week ago. On that day, at 3 p.m., Mrs. Barrows had bounced into his office. "Boo!" she had yelled. "Are you scraping around the bottom of the pickle barrel?" Mr. Martin had looked at her from under his green eyeshade, saying nothing. She had begun to wander about the office, taking it in with her great, popping eyes. "Do you really need *all* these filing cabinets?" she had demanded suddenly. Mr. Martin's heart had jumped. "Each of these files," he had said, keeping his voice even, "plays an indispensable part in the system of F & S." She had brayed at him, "Well, don't tear up the pea patch!" and gone to the door. From there she had bawled, "But you sure have got a lot of fine scrap in here!" Mr. Martin could no longer doubt that the finger was on his beloved department. Her pickaxe was on the upswing, poised for the first blow. It had not come yet; he had received no blue memo from the enchanted Mr. Fitweiler bearing nonsensical instructions deriving from the obscene woman. But there was no doubt in Mr. Martin's mind that one would be forthcoming. He must act quickly. Already a precious week had gone by. Mr. Martin stood up in his living room, still holding his milk glass. "Gentlemen of the jury," he said to himself, "I demand the death penalty for this horrible person."

The next day Mr. Martin followed his routine, as usual. He polished his glasses more often and once sharpened an already sharp pencil, but not even Miss Paird noticed. Only once did he catch sight of his victim; she swept past him in the hall with a patronizing "Hi!" At five-thirty he walked home, as usual, and had a glass of milk, as usual. He had never drunk anything stronger in his life—unless you could count ginger ale. The late Sam Schlosser, the S of F & S, had praised Mr. Martin at a staff meeting several years before for his temperate habits. "Our most efficient worker neither drinks nor smokes," he had said. "The results speak for themselves." Mr. Fitweiler had sat by, nodding approval.

Mr. Martin was still thinking about that red-letter day as he walked over to the Schrafft's on Fifth Avenue near Forty-Sixth Street. He got there, as he always did, at eight o'clock. He finished his dinner and the financial page of the *Sun* at a quarter to nine, as he always did. It was his custom after dinner to take a walk. This time he walked down Fifth Avenue at a casual pace. His gloved hands felt moist and warm, his forehead cold. He transferred the Camels from his overcoat to a jacket pocket. He wondered, as he did so, if they did not represent an unnecessary note of strain. Mrs. Barrows smoked only Luckies. It was his idea to puff a few puffs on a Camel (after the rubbing-out), stub it out in the ashtray holding her lipstick-stained Luckies, and thus drag a small red herring across the trail. Perhaps it was not a good idea. It would take time. He might even choke, too loudly.

Mr. Martin had never seen the house on West Twelfth Street where Mrs. Barrows lived, but he had a clear enough picture of it. Fortunately, she had bragged to everybody about her ducky first-floor apartment in the perfectly darling three-story red-brick. There would be no doorman or other attendants; just the tenants of the second and third floors. As he walked along, Mr. Martin realized that he would get there before nine-thirty. He had considered walking north on Fifth Avenue from Schrafft's to a point from which it would take him until ten o'clock to reach the house. At that hour people were less likely to be coming in or going out. But the procedure would have made an awkward loop in the straight thread of his casualness, and he had abandoned it. It was impossible to figure when people would be entering or leaving the house, anyway. There was a great risk at any hour. If he ran into anybody, he would simply have to place the rubbing-out of Ulgine Barrows in the inactive file forever. The same thing would hold true if there were someone in her apartment. In that case he would just say that he had been passing by,

" What's after you? You're as jumpy as a goat."

recognized her charming house, and thought to drop in.

It was eighteen minutes after nine when Mr. Martin turned into Twelfth Street. A man passed him, and a man and a woman, talking. There was no one within fifty paces when he came to the house, halfway down the block. He was up the steps and in the small vestibule in no time, pressing the bell under the card that said "Mrs. Ulgine Barrows." When the clicking in the lock started, he jumped forward against the door. He got inside fast, closing the door behind him. A bulb in a lantern hung from the hall ceiling on a chain seemed to give a monstrously bright light. There was nobody on the stair, which went up ahead of him along the left wall. A door opened down the hall in the wall on the right. He went toward it swiftly, on tiptoe.

"Well, for God's sake, look who's here!" bawled Mrs. Barrows, and her braying laugh rang out like the report of a shotgun. He rushed past her like a football tackle, bumping her. "Hey, quit shoving!" she said, closing the door behind them. They were in her living room, which seemed to Mr. Martin to be lighted by a hundred lamps. "What's after you?" she said. "You're as jumpy as a goat." He found he was unable to speak. His heart was wheezing in his throat. "I—yes," he finally brought out. She was jabbering and laughing as she started to help him off with his coat. "No, no," he said. "I'll put it here." He took it off and put it on a chair near the door. "Your hat and gloves, too," she said. "You're in a lady's house." He put his hat on top of the coat. Mrs. Barrows seemed larger than he had thought. He kept his gloves on. "I was passing by," he said. "I recognized—is there anyone here?" She laughed louder than ever. "No," she said, "we're all alone. You're as white as a sheet, you funny man. Whatever *has* come over you? I'll mix you a toddy." She started toward a door across the room. "Scotch-and-soda be all right? But say, you don't drink, do you?" She turned and gave him her amused look. Mr. Martin pulled himself together. "Scotch-and-soda will be all right," he heard himself say. He could hear her laughing in the kitchen.

Mr. Martin looked quickly around the living room for the weapon. He had counted on finding one there. There were andirons and a poker and something in a corner that looked like an Indian club. None of them would do. It couldn't be that way. He began to pace around. He came to a desk. On it lay a metal paper knife with an ornate handle. Would it be sharp enough? He reached for it and knocked over a small brass jar. Stamps spilled out of it and it fell to the floor with a clatter. "Hey," Mrs. Barrows yelled from the kitchen, "are you tearing up the pea patch?" Mr. Martin gave a strange laugh. Picking up the knife, he tried its point against his left wrist. It was blunt. It wouldn't do.

When Mrs. Barrows reappeared, carrying two highballs, Mr. Martin, standing there with his gloves on, became acutely conscious of the fantasy he had wrought. Cigarettes in his pocket, a drink prepared for him— it was all too grossly improbable. It was more than that; it was impossible. Somewhere in the back of his mind a vague idea stirred, sprouted. "For heaven's sake, take off those gloves," said Mrs. Barrows. "I always wear them in the house," said Mr. Martin. The idea began to bloom, strange and wonderful. She put the glasses on a coffee table in front of a sofa and sat on the sofa. "Come over here, you odd little man," she said. Mr. Martin went over and sat beside her. It was difficult getting a cigarette out of the pack of Camels, but he managed it. She held a match for him, laughing. "Well," she said, handing him his drink, "this is perfectly marvelous. You with a drink and a cigarette."

Mr. Martin puffed, not too awkwardly, and took a gulp of the highball. "I drink and smoke all the time," he said. He clinked his glass against hers. "Here's nuts to that old windbag, Fitweiler," he said, and gulped again. The stuff tasted awful, but he made no grimace. "Really, Mr. Martin," she said, her voice and posture changing, "you are insulting our employer." Mrs. Barrows was now all special adviser to the president. "I am preparing a bomb," said Mr. Martin, "which will blow the old goat higher than hell." He had only had a little of the drink, which was not strong. It couldn't be that. "Do you take dope or something?" Mrs. Barrows asked coldly. "Heroin," said Mr. Martin. "I'll be coked to the gills when I bump that old buzzard off." "Mr. Martin!" she shouted, getting to her feet. "That will be all of that. You must go at once." Mr. Martin took another swallow of his drink. He tapped his cigarette out in the ashtray and put the pack of Camels on the coffee table. Then he got up. She stood glaring at him. He walked over and put on his hat and coat. "Not a word about this," he said, and laid an index finger against his lips. All Mrs. Barrows could bring out was "Really!" Mr. Martin put his hand on the doorknob. "I'm sitting in the catbird seat," he said. He stuck his tongue out at her and left. Nobody saw him go.

Mr. Martin got to his apartment, walking, well before eleven. No one saw him go in. He had two glasses of milk after brushing his teeth, and he felt elated. It wasn't tipsiness, because he hadn't been tipsy. Anyway, the walk had worn off all effects of the whiskey. He got in bed and read a magazine for a while. He was asleep before midnight.

Mr. Martin got to the office at eight-thirty the next morning, as usual. At a quarter to nine, Ulgine Barrows, who had never before arrived at work before ten, swept into his office. "I'm reporting to Mr. Fitweiler now!" she shouted. "If he turns you over to the police, it's no more than you deserve!" Mr. Martin gave her a look of shocked surprise. "I beg your pardon?" he said. Mrs. Barrows snorted and bounced out of the room, leaving Miss Paird and Joey Hart staring after her. "What's the matter with that old devil now?" asked Miss Paird. "I have no idea," said Mr. Martin, resuming his work. The other two looked at him and then at each other. Miss Paird got up and went out. She walked slowly past the closed door of Mr. Fitweiler's office. Mrs. Barrows was yelling inside, but she was not braying. Miss

Paird could not hear what the woman was saying. She went back to her desk.

Forty-five minutes later, Mrs. Barrows left the president's office and went into her own, shutting the door. It wasn't until half an hour later that Mr. Fitweiler sent for Mr. Martin. The head of the filing department, neat, quiet, attentive, stood in front of the old man's desk. Mr. Fitweiler was pale and nervous. He took his glasses off and twiddled them. He made a small, bruffing sound in his throat. "Martin," he said, "you have been with us more than twenty years." "Twenty-two, sir," said Mr. Martin. "In that time," pursued the president, "your work and your—uh—manner have been exemplary."[2] "I trust so, sir," said Mr. Martin. "I have understood, Martin," said Mr. Fitweiler, "that you have never taken a drink or smoked." "That is correct, sir," said Mr. Martin. "Ah, yes." Mr. Fitweiler polished his glasses. "You may describe what you did after leaving the office yesterday, Martin," he said. Mr. Martin allowed less than a second for his bewildered pause. "Certainly, sir," he said. "I walked home. Then I went to Schrafft's for dinner. Afterward I walked home again. I went to bed early, sir, and read a magazine for a while. I was asleep before eleven." "Ah, yes," said Mr. Fitweiler again. He was silent for a moment, searching for the proper words to say to the head of the filing department. "Mrs. Barrows," he said finally, "Mrs. Barrows has worked hard, Martin, very hard. It grieves me

---

2. **exemplary:** admirable.

"I'm reporting to Mr. Fitweiler now!"

to report that she has suffered a severe breakdown. It has taken the form of a persecution complex[3] accompanied by distressing hallucinations." "I am very sorry, sir," said Mr. Martin. "Mrs. Barrows is under the delusion," continued Mr. Fitweiler, "that you visited her last evening and behaved yourself in an—uh—unseemly manner." He raised his hand to silence Mr. Martin's little pained outcry. "It is the nature of these psychological diseases," Mr. Fitweiler said, "to fix upon the least likely and most innocent party as the—uh—source of persecution. These matters are not for the lay mind to grasp, Martin. I've just had my psychiatrist, Doctor Fitch, on the phone. He would not, of course, commit himself, but he made enough generalizations to substantiate my suspicions. I suggested to Mrs.

Barrows, when she had completed her—uh—story to me this morning, that she visit Doctor Fitch, for I suspected a condition at once. She flew, I regret to say, into a rage, and demanded—uh—requested that I call you on the carpet. You may not know, Martin, but Mrs. Barrows had planned a reorganization of your department—subject to my approval, of course, subject to my approval. This brought you, rather than anyone else, to her mind—but again that is a phenomenon for Doctor Fitch and not for us. So, Martin, I am afraid Mrs. Barrows' usefulness here is at an end." "I am dreadfully sorry, sir," said Mr. Martin.

It was at this point that the door to the office blew open with the suddenness of a gas-main explosion

---

3. **persecution complex**: an unreasonable fear of being harmed by others.

and Mrs. Barrows catapulted through it. "Is the little rat denying it?" she screamed. "He can't get away with that!" Mr. Martin got up and moved discreetly to a point beside Mr. Fitweiler's chair. "You drank and smoked at my apartment," she bawled at Mr. Martin, "and you know it! You called Mr. Fitweiler an old windbag and said you were going to blow him up when you got coked to the gills on your heroin!" She stopped yelling to catch her breath and a new glint came into her popping eyes. "If you weren't such a drab, ordinary little man," she said, "I'd think you'd planned it all. Sticking your tongue out, saying you were sitting in the catbird seat, because you thought no one would believe me when I told it! My God, it's really too perfect!" She brayed loudly and hysterically, and the fury was on her again. She glared at Mr. Fitweiler. "Can't you see how he has tricked us, you old fool? Can't you see his little game?" But Mr. Fitweiler had been surreptitiously pressing all the buttons under the top of his desk and

employees of F & S began pouring into the room. "Stockton," said Mr. Fitweiler, "you and Fishbein will take Mrs. Barrows to her home. Mrs. Powell, you will go with them." Stockton, who had played a little football in high school, blocked Mrs. Barrows as she made for Mr. Martin. It took him and Fishbein together to force her out of the door into the hall, crowded with stenographers and office boys. She was still screaming imprecations at Mr. Martin, tangled and contradictory imprecations. The hubbub finally died out down the corridor.

"I regret that this has happened," said Mr. Fitweiler. "I shall ask you to dismiss it from your mind, Martin." "Yes, sir," said Mr. Martin, anticipating his chief's "That will be all" by moving to the door. "I will dismiss it." He went out and shut the door, and his step was light and quick in the hall. When he entered his department he had slowed down to his customary gait, and he walked quietly across the room to the W20 file, wearing a look of studious concentration.

How important are families to people? In this short story, the narrator befriends a 12-year-old named Jerry who chops wood and does other odd jobs for her. Jerry lives in an orphanage high in the Carolina mountains. Read to find out how important a family is to Jerry.

A Mother in Mannville

Marjorie Kinnan Rawlings (1896–1953)

The orphanage is high in the Carolina mountains. Sometimes in winter the snowdrifts are so deep that the institution is cut off from the village below, from all the world. Fog hides the mountain peaks, the snow swirls down the valleys, and a wind blows so bitterly that the orphanage boys who take the milk twice daily to the baby cottage reach the door with fingers stiff in an agony of numbness.

"Or when we carry trays from the cookhouse for the ones that are sick," Jerry said, "we get our faces frostbit, because we can't put our hands over them. I have gloves," he added. "Some of the boys don't have any."

He liked the late spring, he said. The rhododendron was in bloom, a carpet of color, across the mountainsides, soft as the May winds that stirred the hemlocks. He called it laurel.

"It's pretty when the laurel blooms," he said. "Some of it's pink and some of it's white."

I was there in autumn. I wanted quiet, isolation, to do some troublesome writing. I wanted mountain air to blow out the malaria[1] from too long a time in the subtropics. I was homesick, too, for the flaming of maples in October, and for corn shocks and

---

1. **malaria**: a disease marked by chills and fever that is spread by mosquitoes.

pumpkins and black-walnut trees and the lift of hills. I found them all, living in a cabin that belonged to the orphanage, half a mile beyond the orphanage farm. When I took the cabin, I asked for a boy or man to come and chop wood for the fireplace. The first few days were warm, I found what wood I needed about the cabin, no one came, and I forgot the order.

I looked up from my typewriter one late afternoon, a little startled. A boy stood at the door, and my pointer dog, my companion, was at his side and had not barked to warn me. The boy was probably twelve years old, but under-sized. He wore overalls and a torn shirt, and was barefooted.

He said, "I can chop some wood today."

I said, "But I have a boy coming from the orphanage."

"I'm the boy."

"You? But you're small."

"Size don't matter, chopping wood," he said. "Some of the big boys don't chop good. I've been chopping wood at the orphanage a long time."

I visualized mangled and inade-quate branches for my fires. I was well into my work and not inclined to conversation. I was a little blunt.

"Very well. There's the ax. Go ahead and see what you can do."

I went back to work, closing the door. At first the sound of the boy dragging brush annoyed me. Then he began to chop. The blows were rhythmic and steady, and shortly I had forgotten him, the sound no more of an interruption than a consistent rain. I

suppose an hour and a half passed, for when I stopped and stretched, and heard the boy's steps on the cabin stoop, the sun was dropping behind the farthest mountain, and the valleys were purple with something deeper than the asters.

The boy said, "I have to go to supper now. I can come again tomorrow evening."

I said, "I'll pay you now for what you've done," thinking I should probably have to insist on an older boy. "Ten cents an hour?"

"Anything is all right."

We went together back of the cabin. An astonishing amount of solid wood had been cut. There were cherry logs and heavy roots of rhododendron, and blocks from the waste pine and oak left from the building of the cabin.

"But you've done as much as a man," I said. "This is a splendid pile."

I looked at him, actually, for the first time. His hair was the color of the corn shocks, and his eyes, very direct, were like the mountain sky when rain is pending—gray, with a showing of that miraculous blue. As I spoke a light came over him, as though the setting sun had touched him with the same suffused glory with which it touched the mountains. I gave him a quarter.

"You may come tomorrow," I said, "and thank you very much."

He looked at me, and at the coin, and seemed to want to speak, but could not, and turned away.

"I'll split the kindling tomorrow," he said over his thin ragged shoulder. "You'll need kindling and medium

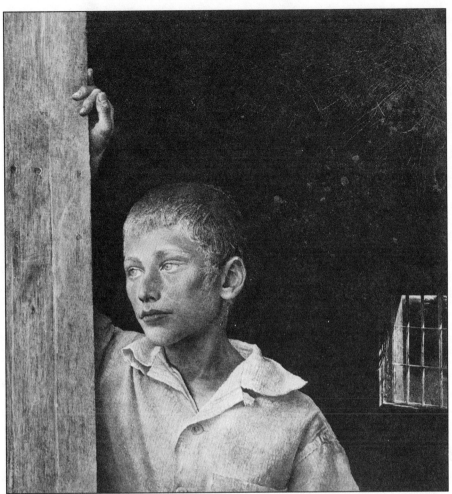

ALBERT'S SON, 1959, Andrew Wyeth, National Museum of Contemporary Art, Oslo, Norway, courtesy Frank E. Fowler

wood and logs and backlogs."

At daylight I was half awakened by the sound of chopping. Again it was so even in texture that I went back to sleep. When I left my bed in the cool morning, the boy had come and gone, and a stack of kindling was neat against the cabin wall. He came again after school in the afternoon and worked until time to return to the orphanage. His name was Jerry; he was twelve years old, and he had been at the orphanage since he was four. I could picture him at four, with the same grave gray-blue eyes and the same—independence? No, the word that comes to me is "integrity."[2]

The word means something very special to me, and the quality for which I use it is a rare one. My father had it—there is another of whom I am almost sure—but almost no man of my acquaintance possesses it with the clarity, the purity, the simplicity of a mountain stream. But the boy Jerry had it. It is bedded on courage, but it is

---

2. integrity: sincerity and honesty.

more than brave. It is honest, but it is more than honesty. The ax handle broke one day. Jerry said the woodshop at the orphanage would repair it. I brought money to pay for the job and he refused it.

"I'll pay for it," he said, "I broke it. I brought the ax down careless."

"But no one hits accurately every time," I told him. "The fault was in the wood of the handle. I'll see the man from whom I bought it."

It was only then that he would take the money. He was standing back of his own carelessness. He was a free-will agent and he chose to do careful work, and if he failed, he took the responsibility without subterfuge.[3]

And he did for me the unnecessary thing, the gracious thing, that we find done only by the great of heart. Things no training can teach, for they are done on the instant, with no predicated experience. He found a cubbyhole beside the fireplace that I had not noticed. There, of his own accord, he put kindling and "medium" wood, so that I might always have dry fire material ready in case of sudden wet weather. A stone was loose in the rough walk to the cabin. He dug a deeper hole and steadied it, although he came, himself, by a shortcut over the bank. I found that when I tried to return his thoughtfulness with such things as candy and apples, he was wordless. "Thank you" was, perhaps, an expression for which he had had no use, for his courtesy was instinctive. He only looked at the gift and at me, and a curtain lifted, so that I saw deep into the clear well of his eyes, and gratitude was there, and affection, soft over the firm granite of his character.

He made simple excuses to come and sit with me. I could no more have turned him away than if he had been physically hungry. I suggested once that the best time for us to visit was just before supper, when I left off my writing. After that, he waited always until my typewriter had been some time quiet. One day I worked until nearly dark. I went outside the cabin, having forgotten him. I saw him going up over the hill in the twilight toward the orphanage. When I sat down on my stoop, a place was warm from his body where he had been sitting.

He became initimate, of course, with my pointer, Pat. There is a strange communion between a boy and a dog. Perhaps they possess the same singleness of spirit, the same kind of wisdom. It is difficult to explain, but it exists. When I went across the state for a weekend I left the dog in Jerry's charge. I gave him the dog whistle and the key to the cabin, and left sufficient food. He was to come two or three times a day and let out the dog, and feed and exercise him. I should return Sunday night, and Jerry would take out the dog for the last time Sunday afternoon and then leave the key under an agreed hiding place.

My return was belated and fog filled the mountain passes so treacherously that I dared not drive at night. The fog held the next morning, and it was Monday noon before I reached the

---

3. subterfuge: a trick to avoid unpleasantness.

cabin. The dog had been fed and cared for that morning. Jerry came early in the afternoon, anxious.

"The superintendent said nobody would drive in the fog," he said. "I came just before bedtime last night and you hadn't come. So I brought Pat some of my breakfast this morning. I wouldn't have let anything happen to him."

"I was sure of that. I didn't worry."

"When I heard about the fog, I thought you'd know."

He was needed for work at the orphanage and he had to return at once. I gave him a dollar in payment, and he looked at it and went away. But that night he came in the darkness and knocked at the door.

"Come in, Jerry," I said, "if you're allowed to be away this late."

"I told maybe a story," he said, "I told them I thought you would want to see me."

"That's true," I assured him, and I saw his relief. "I want to hear about how you managed with the dog."

He sat by the fire with me, with no other light, and told me of their two days together. The dog lay close to him, and found a comfort there that I did not have for him. And it seemed to me that being with my dog, and caring for him, had brought the boy and me, too, together, so that he felt that he belonged to me as well as to the animal.

"He stayed right with me," he told me, "except when he ran in the laurel. He likes the laurel. I took him up over the hill and we both ran fast. There was a place where the grass was high and I

lay down in it and hid. I could hear Pat hunting for me. He found my trail and he barked. When he found me, he acted crazy, and he ran around and around me, in circles."

We watched the flames.

"That's an apple log," he said. "It burns the prettiest of any wood."

We were very close.

He was suddenly impelled to speak of things he had not spoken of before, nor had I cared to ask him.

"You look a little bit like my mother," he said. "Especially in the dark, by the fire."

"But you were only four, Jerry, when you came here. You have remembered how she looked, all these years?"

"My mother lives in Mannville," he said.

For a moment, finding that he had a mother shocked me as greatly as anything in my life has ever done, and I did not know why it disturbed me. Then I understood my distress. I was filled with a passionate resentment that any woman should go away and leave her son. A fresh anger added itself. A son like this one— The orphanage was a wholesome place, the executives were kind, good people, the food was more than adequate, the boys were healthy, a ragged shirt was no hardship, nor the doing of clean labor. Granted, perhaps, that the boy felt no lack, what about the mother? At four he would have looked the same as now. Nothing, I thought, nothing in life could change those eyes. His quality must be apparent to an idiot, a fool. I burned with questions I could not ask. In any, I was afraid, there would be pain.

"Have you seen her, Jerry—lately?"

"I see her every summer. She sends for me."

I wanted to cry out. "Why are you not with her? How can she let you go away again?"

He said, "She comes up here from Mannville whenever she can. She doesn't have a job now."

His face shone in the firelight.

"She wanted to give me a puppy, but they can't let any one boy keep a puppy. You remember the suit I had on last Sunday?" He was plainly proud. "She sent me that for Christmas. The Christmas before that"—he drew a long breath, savoring the memory— "she sent me a pair of skates."

"Roller skates?"

My mind was busy, making pictures of her, trying to understand her. She had not, then, entirely deserted or forgotten him. But why, then— I thought, "But I must not condemn her without knowing."

"Roller skates. I let the other boys use them. They're always borrowing them. But they're careful of them."

What circumstance other than poverty—

"I'm going to take the dollar you gave me for taking care of Pat," he said, "and buy her a pair of gloves."

I could only say, "That will be nice. Do you know her size?"

"I think it's eight and a half," he said.

He looked at my hands.

"Do you wear eight and a half?" he asked.

"No. I wear a smaller size, a six."

"Oh! Then I guess her hands are bigger than yours."

I hated her. Poverty or no, there was other food than bread, and the soul could starve as quickly as the body. He was taking his dollar to buy gloves for her big stupid hands, and she lived away from him, in Mannville, and contented herself with sending him skates.

"She likes white gloves," he said. "Do you think I can get them for a dollar?"

"I think so," I said.

I decided that I should not leave the mountains without seeing her and knowing for myself why she had done this thing.

The human mind scatters its interests as though made of thistle-down, and every wind stirs and moves it. I finished my work. It did not please me, and I gave my thoughts to another field. I should need some Mexican material.

I made arrangements to close my Florida place. Mexico immediately, and doing the writing there, if conditions were favorable. Then, Alaska with my brother. After that, heaven knew what or where.

I did not take time to go to Mannville to see Jerry's mother, nor even to talk with the orphanage officials about her. I was a trifle abstracted[4] about the boy, because of

---

4. abstracted: absent-minded.

my work and plans. And after my first fury at her—we did not speak of her again—his having a mother, any sort at all, not far away, in Mannville, relieved me of the ache I had had about him. He did not question the anomalous[5] relation. He was not lonely. It was none of my concern.

He came every day and cut my wood and did small helpful favors and stayed to talk. The days had become cold, and often I let him come inside the cabin. He would lie on the floor in front of the fire, with one arm across the pointer, and they would both doze and wait quietly for me. Other days they ran with a common ecstasy through the laurel, and since the asters were now gone, he brought me back vermilion maple leaves, and chestnut boughs dripping with imperial yellow. I was ready to go.

I said to him, "You have been my good friend, Jerry. I shall often think of you and miss you. Pat will miss you too. I am leaving tomorrow."

He did not answer. When he went away, I remember that a new moon hung over the mountains, and I watched him go in silence up the hill. I expected him the next day, but he did not come. The details of packing my personal belongings, loading my car, arranging the bed over the seat, where the dog would ride, occupied me until late in the day. I closed the cabin and started the car, noticing that the sun was in the west and I should do well to be out of the mountains by nightfall. I stopped by the orphanage and left the cabin key and money for my light bill with Miss Clark.

"And will you call Jerry for me to say good-by to him?"

"I don't know where he is," she said. "I'm afraid he's not well. He didn't eat his dinner this noon. One of the boys saw him going over the hill into the laurel. He was supposed to fire the boiler this afternoon. It's not like him; he's unusually reliable."

I was almost relieved, for I knew I should never see him again, and it would be easier not to say good-by to him.

I said, "I wanted to talk with you about his mother—why he's here—but I'm in more of a hurry than I expected to be. It's out of the question for me to see her now. But here's some money I'd like to leave with you to buy things for him at Christmas and on his birthday. It will be better than for me to try to send him things. I could so easily duplicate—skates, for instance."

She blinked her honest spinster's eyes.

"There's not much use for skates here," she said.

Her stupidity annoyed me.

"What I mean," I said, "is that I don't want to duplicate things his mother sends him. I might have chosen skates if I didn't know she had already given them to him."

"I don't understand," she said. "He has no mother. He has no skates."

---

5. anomalous: unusual.

Have you ever found yourself in an ordinary situation that turned into something quite unusual? Stranded on a cold, windy night, the narrator sees a lamp in a window of a small house. Its elderly owner welcomes him, and the two enjoy pleasant conversation. Read to find out the strange discovery the narrator makes about this kindly old woman.

A Lamp in a Window

Truman Capote (1924–1984)

Once I was invited to a wedding; the bride suggested I drive up from New York with a pair of other guests, a Mr. and Mrs. Roberts whom I had never met before. It was a cold April day, and on the ride to Connecticut the Robertses, a couple in their early forties, seemed agreeable enough—no one you would want to spend a long weekend with, but not bad.

However, at the wedding reception a great deal of liquor was consumed, I should say a third of it by my chauffeurs. They were the last to leave the party—at approximately 11 p.m.—and I was most wary of accompanying them; I knew they were drunk, but I didn't realize how drunk. We had driven about twenty miles, the car weaving considerably, and Mr. and Mrs. Roberts were insulting each other in the most extraordinary language (really, it was a moment out of *Who's Afraid of Virginia Woolf?*), when Mr. Roberts, very understandably, made a wrong turn and got lost on a dark country road. I kept asking them, finally begging them to stop the car and let me out, but they were so involved in their invectives[1] that they ignored me. Eventually the car stopped of its own accord (temporarily) when it swiped against the side of a tree. I used

---
1. **invectives:** harsh words.

the opportunity to jump out of the car's back door and run into the woods. Presently the cursed vehicle drove off, leaving me alone in the icy dark. I'm sure my hosts never missed me; Lord knows I didn't miss them.

But it wasn't a joy to be stranded out there on a windy, cold night. I started walking, hoping I'd reach a highway. I walked for half an hour without sighting a habitation. Then just off the road, I saw a small frame cottage with a porch and a window lighted by a lamp. I tiptoed onto the porch and looked in the window; an elderly woman with soft white hair and a round pleasant face was sitting by a fireside reading a book. There was a cat curled in her lap, and several others slumbering at her feet.

I knocked at the door, and when she opened it I said, with chattering teeth, "I'm sorry to disturb you, but I've had a sort of accident. I wonder if I could use your phone to call a taxi."

"Oh, dear," she said smiling. "I'm afraid I don't have a phone. Too poor. But please, come in." And as I stepped through the door into the cozy room, she said: "My goodness, boy. You're freezing. Can I make coffee? A cup of tea? I have a little whiskey my husband left—he died six years ago."

I said a little whiskey would be very welcome.

While she fetched it I warmed my hands at the fire and glanced around the room. It was a cheerful place occupied by six or seven cats of varying alley-cat colors. I looked at the title of the book Mrs. Kelly—for that was her

name, as I later learned—had been reading: it was *Emma* by Jane Austen, a favorite of mine.

When Mrs. Kelly returned with a glass of ice and a dusty quarter-bottle of bourbon, she said: "Sit down, sit down. It's not often I have company. Of course, I have my cats. Anyway, you'll spend the night? I have a nice little guest room that's been waiting such a long time for a guest. In the morning you can walk to the highway and catch a ride into town where you'll find a garage to fix your car. It's about five miles away."

I wondered aloud how she could live so isolatedly, without transportation or a telephone; she told me her good friend, the mailman, took care of all her shopping needs. "Albert. He's really so dear and faithful. But he's due to retire next year. After that I don't know what I'll do. But something will turn up. Perhaps a kindly new mailman. Tell me, just what sort of accident did you have?"

When I explained the truth of the matter, she responded indignantly: "You did exactly the right thing. I wouldn't set foot in a car with a man who had sniffed a glass of sherry. That's how I lost my husband. Married forty years, forty happy years, and I lost him because a drunken driver ran him down. If it wasn't for my cats..." She stroked an orange tabby purring in her lap.

We talked by the fire until my eyes grew heavy. We talked about Jane Austen ("Ah, Jane. My tragedy is that I've read all her books so often I have them memorized"), and other admired authors: Thoreau, Willa Cather, Dickens, Lewis Carroll, Agatha Christie, Raymond Chandler, Hawthorne, Chekhov, De Maupassant—she was a woman with a good and varied mind; intelligence illuminated her hazel eyes like the small lamp shining on the table beside her. We talked about the hard Connecticut winters, politicians, far places ("I've never been abroad, but if ever I'd had the chance, the place I would have gone is Africa. Sometimes I've dreamed of it, the green hills, the heat, the beautiful giraffes, the elephants walking about"), religion ("Of course, I was raised a Catholic, but now, I'm sorry to say, I have an open mind. Too much reading, perhaps"), gardening ("I grow and can all my own vegetables, a necessity"). At last: "Forgive my babbling on. You have no idea how much pleasure it gives me. But it's way past your bedtime. I know it is mine."

She escorted me upstairs, and after I was comfortably arranged in a double bed under a blissful load of pretty scrap quilts, she returned to wish me good-night, sweet dreams. I lay awake thinking about it. What an exceptional experience—to be an old woman living alone here in the wilderness and have a stranger knock on your door in the middle of the night and not only open it but warmly welcome him inside and offer him shelter. If our situation had been reversed, I doubt that I would have had the courage, to say nothing of the generosity.

The next morning she gave me breakfast in her kitchen. Coffee and hot oatmeal with sugar and tinned cream, but I was hungry and it tasted great. The kitchen was shabbier than the rest of the house; the stove, a rattling refrigerator, everything seemed on the edge of expiring. All except one large, somewhat modern object, a deep-freeze that fitted into a corner of the room.

She was chatting on: "I love birds. I feel so guilty about not tossing them crumbs during the winter. But I can't have them gathering around the house. Because of the cats. Do you care for cats?"

"Yes, I once had a Siamese named Toma. She lived to be twelve, and we traveled everywhere together. All over the world. And when she died I never had the heart to get another."

"Then maybe you will understand this," she said, leading me over to the deep-freeze, and opening it. Inside was nothing but cats: stacks of frozen, perfectly preserved cats—dozens of them. It gave me an odd sensation. "All my old friends. Gone to rest. It's just that I couldn't bear to lose them. *Completely*." She laughed and said: "I guess you think I'm a bit dotty."

A bit dotty. Yes, a bit dotty, I thought as I walked under grey skies in the direction of the highway she had pointed out to me. But radiant: a lamp in a window.

What would you do if you were unjustly convicted of a crime? In this Russian short story, the main character Ivan Dmitrich Aksionov spends 26 years in prison for a murder he did not commit. Read to find out where Aksionov found the strength to endure such injustice.

God Sees the Truth, But Waits

Leo N. Tolstoy (1828–1910)

In the town of Vladimir lived a young merchant named Ivan Dmitrich Aksionov. He had two shops and a house of his own.

Aksionov was a handsome, fair-haired, curly-headed fellow, full of fun, and very fond of singing. When quite a young man he had been given to drink, and was riotous when he had had too much; but after he married he gave up drinking, except now and then.

One summer Aksionov was going to the Nizhny Fair, and as he bade good-bye to his family, his wife said to him, "Ivan Dmitrich, do not start to-day; I have had a bad dream about you."

Aksionov laughed, and said, "You are afraid that when I get to the fair I shall go on a spree."

His wife replied: "I do not know what I am afraid of; all I know is that I had a bad dream. I dreamt you returned from the town, and when you took off your cap I saw that your hair was quite grey."

Aksionov laughed. "That's a lucky sign," said he. "See if I don't sell out all my goods, and bring you some presents from the fair."

So he said good-bye to his family, and drove away.

When he had travelled half-way, he met a merchant whom he knew, and

MY FATHER AT TABLE, 1925, Marc Chagall, copyright 1990 ARS N.Y./ADAGP

they put up at the same inn for the night. They had some tea together, and then went to bed in adjoining rooms.

It was not Aksionov's habit to sleep late, and, wishing to travel while it was still cool, he aroused his driver before dawn, and told him to put in the horses.

Then he made his way across to the landlord of the inn (who lived in a cottage at the back), paid his bill, and continued his journey.

When he had gone about twenty-five miles, he stopped for the horses to be fed. Aksionov rested awhile in the passage of the inn, then he stepped out into the porch, and, ordering a samovar[1] to be heated, got out his guitar and began to play.

Suddenly a troika[2] drove up with tinkling bells and an official alighted, followed by two soldiers. He came to Aksionov and began to question him, asking him who he was and whence he came. Aksionov answered him fully, and said, "Won't you have some tea with me?" But the official went on cross-questioning him and asking him, "Where did you spend last night? Were you alone, or with a fellow-merchant? Did you see the other merchant this morning? Why did you leave the inn before dawn?"

Aksionov wondered why he was asked all these questions, but he described all that had happened, and

1. **samovar:** Russian teakettle.
2. **troika:** a carriage drawn by three horses.

then added, "Why do you cross-question me as if I were a thief or a robber? I am travelling on business of my own, and there is no need to question me."

Then the official, calling the soldiers, said, "I am the police-officer of this district, and I question you because the merchant with whom you spent last night has been found with his throat cut. We must search your things."

They entered the house. The soldiers and the police-officer un-strapped Aksionov's luggage and searched it. Suddenly the officer drew a knife out of a bag, crying, "Whose knife is this?"

Aksionov looked, and seeing a blood-stained knife taken from his bag, he was frightened.

"How is it there is blood on this knife?"

Aksionov tried to answer, but could hardly utter a word, and only stammered: "I—don't know—not mine."

Then the police-officer said: "This morning the merchant was found in bed with his throat cut. You are the only person who could have done it. The house was locked from inside, and no one else was there. Here is this blood-stained knife in your bag, and your face and manner betray you! Tell me how you killed him, and how much money you stole?"

Aksionov swore he had not done it; that he had not seen the merchant after they had had tea together; that he had no money except eight thousand rubles of his own, and that the knife was not his. But his voice was broken, his face pale, and he trembled with fear as though he were guilty.

The police-officer ordered the soldiers to bind Aksionov and to put him in the cart. As they tied his feet together and flung him into the cart, Aksionov crossed himself and wept. His money and goods were taken from him, and he was sent to the nearest town and imprisoned there. Enquiries as to his character were made in Vladimir. The merchants and other inhabitants said that in former days he used to drink and waste his time, but that he was a good man. Then the trial came on: he was charged with murdering a merchant from Ryazan, and robbing him of twenty thousand rubles.

His wife was in despair, and did not know what to believe. Her children were all quite small; one was a baby at her breast. Taking them all with her, she went to the town where her husband was in jail. At first she was not allowed to see him; but after much begging, she obtained permission from the officials, and was taken to him. When she saw her husband in prison-dress and in chains, shut up with thieves and criminals, she fell down, and did not come to her senses for a long time. Then she drew her children to her, and sat down near him. She told him of things at home, and asked about what had happened to him. He told her all, and she asked, "What can we do now?"

"We must petition the Czar[3] not to let an innocent man perish."

3. **Czar:** Russian emperor.

His wife told him that she had sent a petition to the Czar, but it had not been accepted.

Aksionov did not reply, but only looked downcast.

Then his wife said, "It was not for nothing I dreamt your hair had turned grey. You remember? You should not have started that day." And passing her fingers through his hair, she said: "Vanya, dearest, tell your wife the truth; was it not you who did it?"

"So you, too, suspect me!" said Aksionov, and, hiding his face in his hands, he began to weep. Then a soldier came to say that the wife and children must go away; and Aksionov said good-bye to his family for the last time.

When they were gone, Aksionov recalled what had been said, and when he remembered that his wife also had suspected him, he said to himself, "It seems that only God can know the truth; it is to Him alone we must appeal, and from Him alone expect mercy."

And Aksionov wrote no more petitions; gave up all hope, and only prayed to God.

Aksionov was condemned to be flogged and sent to the mines. So he was flogged with a knot, and when the wounds made by the knot were healed, he was driven to Siberia[4] with other convicts.

For twenty-six years Aksionov lived as a convict in Siberia. His hair turned white as snow, and his beard grew long, thin, and grey. All his mirth went; he stooped; he walked slowly, spoke little, and never laughed, but he often prayed.

In prison Aksionov learnt to make boots, and earned a little money, with which he bought *The Lives of the Saints*. He read this book when there was light enough in the prison; and on Sundays in the prison-church he read the lessons and sang in the choir; for his voice was still good.

The prison authorities liked Aksionov for his meekness, and his fellow-prisoners respected him: they called him "Grandfather," and "The Saint." When they wanted to petition the prison authorities about anything, they always made Aksionov their spokesman, and when there were quarrels among the prisoners they came to him to put things right, and to judge the matter.

No news reached Aksionov from his home, and he did not even know if his wife and children were still alive.

One day a fresh gang of convicts came to the prison. In the evening the old prisoners collected round the new ones and asked them what towns or villages they came from, and what they were sentenced for. Among the rest Aksionov sat down near the new-comers, and listened with downcast air to what was said.

One of the new convicts, a tall, strong man of sixty, with a closely-cropped grey beard, was telling the others what he had been arrested for.

"Well, friends," he said, "I only took a horse that was tied to a sledge, and I was arrested and accused of

---

4. **Siberia:** cold, northern region of the Soviet Union.

CONVERSATIONS, 1958, Ben Shahn, watercolor on paper, 39¼ x 27 inches. Collection of Whitney Museum of American Art. Purchase, with funds from the Friends of the Whitney Museum of American Art. 58.21

stealing. I said I had only taken it to get home quicker, and had then let it go; besides, the driver was a personal friend of mine. So I said, 'It's all right.' 'No,' said they, 'you stole it.' But how or where I stole it they could not say. I once really did something wrong, and ought by rights to have come here long ago, but that time I was not found out. Now I have been sent here for nothing at all. . . . Eh, but it's lies I'm telling you; I've been to Siberia before, but I did not stay long."

"Where are you from?" asked someone.

"From Vladimir. My family are of that town. My name is Makar, and they also call me Semyonich."

Aksionov raised his head and said: "Tell me, Semyonich, do you know anything of the merchants Aksionov of Vladimir? Are they still alive?"

"Know them? Of course I do. The Aksionovs are rich, though their father is in Siberia: a sinner like ourselves, it seems! As for you, Gran'dad, how did you come here?"

Aksionov did not like to speak of his misfortune. He only sighed, and said, "For my sins I have been in prison these twenty-six years."

"What sins?" asked Makar Semyonich.

But Aksionov only said, "Well, well—I must have deserved it!" He would have said no more, but his companions told the newcomers how Aksionov came to be in Siberia; how someone had killed a merchant, and had put the knife among Aksionov's things, and Aksionov had been unjustly condemned.

When Makar Semyonich heard this, he looked at Aksionov, slapped his own knee, and exclaimed, "Well, this is wonderful! Really wonderful! But how old you've grown, Gran'dad!"

The others asked him why he was so surprised, and where he had seen Aksionov before; but Makar Semyonich did not reply. He only said: "It's wonderful that we should meet here, lads!"

These words made Aksionov wonder whether this man knew who had killed the merchant; so he said, "Perhaps, Semyonich, you have heard of that affair, or maybe you've seen me before?"

"How could I help hearing? The world's full of rumours. But it's a long time ago, and I've forgotten what I heard."

"Perhaps you heard who killed the merchant?" asked Aksionov.

Makar Semyonich laughed and replied: "It must have been him in whose bag the knife was found! If someone else hid the knife there, 'He's not a thief till he's caught,' as the saying is. How could anyone put a knife into your bag while it was under your head? It would surely have woke you up."

When Aksionov heard these words, he felt sure this was the man who had killed the merchant. He rose and went away. All that night Aksionov lay awake. He felt terribly unhappy, and all sorts of images rose in his mind. There was the image of his wife as she was when he parted from her to go to the fair. He saw her as if she were present; her face and her eyes rose before him; he heard her speak and laugh. Then he saw his children, quite little, as they were at that time: one with a little cloak on, another at his mother's breast. And then he remembered himself as he used to be—young and merry. He remembered how he sat playing the guitar in the porch of the inn where he was arrested, and how free from care he had been. He saw, in his mind, the place where he was flogged, the executioner, and the people standing around; the chains, the convicts, all the twenty-six years of his prison life, and his premature old age. The thought of it all made him so wretched that he was ready to kill himself.

"And it's all that villain's doing!" thought Aksionov. And his anger was so great against Makar Semyonich that he longed for vengeance, even if he himself should perish for it. He kept repeating prayers all night, but could get no peace. During the day he did not go near Makar Semyonich, nor even look at him.

A fortnight passed in this way. Aksionov could not sleep at night, and was so miserable that he did not know what to do.

One night as he was walking about the prison he noticed some earth that came rolling out from under one of the shelves on which the prisoners slept. He stopped to see what it was.

Suddenly Makar Semyonich crept out from under the shelf, and looked up at Aksionov with frightened face. Aksionov tried to pass without looking at him, but Makar seized his hand and told him that he had dug a hole under the wall, getting rid of the earth by putting it into his high-boots, and emptying it out every day on the road when the prisoners were driven to their work.

"Just you keep quiet, old man, and you shall get out too. If you blab, they'll flog the life out of me, but I will kill you first."

Aksionov trembled with anger as he looked at his enemy. He drew his hand away, saying, "I have no wish to escape, and you have no need to kill me; you killed me long ago! As to telling of you—I may do so or not, as God shall direct."

Next day, when the convicts were led out to work, the convoy soldiers noticed that one or other of the prisoners emptied some earth out of his boots. The prison was searched and the tunnel found. The Governor came and questioned all the prisoners to find out who had dug the hole. They all denied any knowledge of it. Those who knew would not betray Makar Semyonich, knowing he would be flogged almost to death. At last the Governor turned to Aksionov whom he knew to be a just man, and said: "You are a truthful old man; tell me, before God, who dug the hole?"

Makar Semyonich stood as if he were quite unconcerned, looking at the Governor and not so much as glancing at Aksionov. Aksionov's lips and hands trembled, and for a long time he could not utter a word. He thought, "Why should I screen him who ruined my life? Let him pay for what I have suffered. But if I tell, they will probably flog the life out of him, and maybe I suspect him wrongly. And, after all, what good would it be to me?"

"Well, old man," repeated the Governor, "tell me the truth: who has been digging under the wall?"

Aksionov glanced at Makar Semyonich, and said, "I cannot say, your honour. It is not God's will that I should tell! Do what you like with me; I am in your hands."

However much the Governor tried, Aksionov would say no more, and so the matter had to be left.

That night, when Aksionov was lying on his bed and just beginning to doze, someone came quietly and sat down on his bed. He peered through the darkness and recognized Makar.

"What more do you want of me?" asked Aksionov. "Why have you come here?"

Makar Semyonich was silent. So Aksionov sat up and said, "What do you want? Go away, or I will call the guard!"

Makar Semyonich bent close over Aksionov, and whispered, "Ivan Dmitrich, forgive me!"

"What for?" asked Aksionov.

"It was I who killed the merchant and hid the knife among your things. I meant to kill you too, but I heard a noise outside, so I hid the knife in your bag and escaped out of the window."

Aksionov was silent, and did not know what to say. Makar Semyonich slid off the bed-shelf and knelt upon the ground. "Ivan Dmitrich," said he, "forgive me! For the love of God, forgive me! I will confess that it was I who killed the merchant, and you will be released and can go to your home."

"It is easy for you to talk," said Aksionov, "but I have suffered for you these twenty-six years. Where could I go to now?...My wife is dead, and my children have forgotten me. I have nowhere to go...."

Makar Semyonich did not rise, but beat his head on the floor. "Ivan Dmitrich, forgive me!" he cried. "When they flogged me with the knot it was not so hard to bear as it is to see you now...yet you had pity on me, and did not tell. For Christ's sake forgive me, wretch that I am!" And he began to sob.

When Aksionov heard him sobbing he, too, began to weep. "God will forgive you!" said he. "Maybe I am a hundred times worse than you." And at these words his heart grew light, and the longing for home left him. He no longer had any desire to leave the prison, but only hoped for his last hour to come.

In spite of what Aksionov had said, Makar Semyonich confessed his guilt. But when the order for his release came Aksionov was already dead.

Unit 2: Novels

All good books have one thing in common—
they are truer than if they had really happened.

Ernest Hemingway

Like a short story, a novel contains the elements of setting, character, plot, and theme. But the longer length of novels allows authors to expand on each element in greater depth. The setting may change from place to place, and stretch over many years. Minor characters have an impact on the lives of the one or two main characters. Subplots weave in and out of the novel's main action. The ideas or themes communicated in a novel are often numerous.

Why do people take the time to read novels? There are many reasons. Some novels offer readers an escape from everyday life. Novels can also provide information about or insight into a variety of subjects. Other novels point out problems or injustices that challenge readers to take action. But most people take the time to read novels for a far simpler reason. After just a few pages, readers find themselves thoroughly involved in a good novel. They *must* read on to the end.

Although a novel is imaginary, it may be based on actual events or real people. In the first excerpt, you join young German soldiers during World War I as they visit a dying friend in a field hospital. The author, Erich Maria Remarque, actually fought in this war and was wounded several times. In the second excerpt, you observe the injustice suffered by a poor Mexican family who cannot afford a doctor's services. After you finish each excerpt, you may want to read the entire novel from which it came. Join the millions of people who have enjoyed these popular novels.

The horrors of war were well known to Erich Maria Remarque, the author of this novel. Born in Germany, he fought for his country in World War I and was wounded several times. Remarque continued writing about war's destruction long after he left Germany and settled in the United States.

The Western Front refers to the battlefield between Germany and France during World War I from 1914 to 1918. In this excerpt from the novel, the narrator and three fellow soldiers—Katczinsky, Müller, and Kropp—visit a badly wounded friend in a field hospital. As you read, imagine you are with these young men on a battlefield far from home.

From

All Quiet on the Western Front

Erich Maria Remarque (1898–1970)

Kantorek had been our schoolmaster, a stern little man in a grey tail-coat, with a face like a shrew mouse. He was about the same size as Corporal Himmelstoss, the "terror of Klosterberg." It is very queer that the unhappiness of the world is so often brought on by small men. They are so much more energetic and uncompromising than the big fellows. I have always taken good care to keep out of sections with small company commanders. They are mostly confounded little martinets.[1]

During drill-time Kantorek gave us long lectures until the whole of our class went, under his shepherding, to the District Commandant and volunteered. I can see him now, as he used to glare at us through his spectacles and say in a moving voice: "Won't you join up, Comrades?"

These teachers always carry their feelings ready in their waistcoat pockets, and trot them out by the hour. But we didn't think of that then.

----

1. martinets: strict disciplinarians.

There was, indeed, one of us who hesitated and did not want to fall into line. That was Joseph Behm, a plump, homely fellow. But he did allow himself to be persuaded, otherwise he would have been ostracized.[2] And perhaps more of us thought as he did, but no one could very well stand out, because at that time even one's parents were ready with the word "coward"; no one had the vaguest idea what we were in for. The wisest were just the poor and simple people. They knew the war to be a misfortune, whereas those who were better off, and should have been able to see more clearly what the consequences would be, were beside themselves with joy.

Katczinsky said that was a result of their upbringing. It made them stupid. And what Kat said, he had thought about.

Strange to say, Behm was one of the first to fall. He got hit in the eye during an attack, and we left him lying for dead. We couldn't bring him with us, because we had to come back helter-skelter. In the afternoon suddenly we heard him call, and saw him crawling about in No Man's Land. He had only been knocked unconscious. Because he could not see, and was mad with pain, he failed to keep under cover, and so was shot down before anyone could go and fetch him in.

Naturally we couldn't blame Kantorek for this. Where would the world be if one brought every man to book? There were thousands of Kantoreks, all of whom were convinced that they were acting for the best—in a way that cost them nothing.

And that is why they let us down so badly.

For us lads of eighteen they ought to have been mediators and guides to the world of maturity, the world of work, of duty, of culture, of progress—to the future. We often made fun of them and played jokes on them, but in our hearts we trusted them. The idea

---

2. **ostracized:** cast out of a group.

of authority, which they represented, was associated in our minds with a greater insight and a more humane wisdom. But the first death we saw shattered this belief. We had to recognize that our generation was more to be trusted than theirs. They surpassed us only in phrases and in cleverness. The first bombardment showed us our mistake, and under it the world as they had taught it to us broke in pieces.

While they continued to write and talk, we saw the wounded and dying. While they taught that duty to one's country is the greatest thing, we already knew that death-throes are stronger. But for all that we were no mutineers, no deserters, no cowards—they were very free with all these expressions. We loved our country as much as they; we went courageously into every action; but also we distinguished the false from true, we had suddenly learned to see. And we saw that there was nothing of their world left. We were all at once terribly alone; and alone we must see it through.

Before going over to see Kemmerich we pack up his things: he will need them on the way back.

In the dressing station there is great activity: it reeks as ever of carbolic, pus, and sweat. We are accustomed to a good deal in the billets,[3] but this makes us feel faint. We ask for Kemmerich. He lies in a large room and receives us with feeble expressions of joy and helpless agitation. While he was unconscious someone had stolen his watch.

UPI/Bettmann Newsphotos

Müller shakes his head: "I always told you that nobody should carry as good a watch as that."

Müller is rather crude and tactless, otherwise he would hold his tongue, for anybody can see that Kemmerich will never come out of this place again. Whether he finds his watch or not will make no difference; at the most one will only be able to send it to his people.

"How goes it, Franz?" asks Kropp.

Kemmerich's head sinks.

"Not so bad . . . but I have such a damned pain in my foot."

We look at his bed covering. His leg lies under a wire basket. The bed covering arches over it. I kick Müller on the shin, for he is just about to tell Kemmerich what the orderlies told us outside: that Kemmerich has lost his foot. The leg is amputated. He looks ghastly, yellow and wan. In his face there are already the strained lines that we know so well, we have seen them now hundreds of times. They are not

---

3. billets: housing for troops.

so much lines as marks. Under the skin the life no longer pulses, it has already pressed out the boundaries of the body. Death is working through from within. It already has command in the eyes. Here lies our comrade, Kemmerich, who a little while ago was roasting horseflesh with us and squatting in the shell-holes. He it is still and yet it is not he any longer. His features have become uncertain and faint, like a photographic plate from which two pictures have been taken. Even his voice sounds like ashes.

I think of the time when we went away. His mother, a good plump matron, brought him to the station. She wept continually, her face was bloated and swollen. Kemmerich felt embarrassed, for she was the least composed of all; she simply dissolved into fat and water. Then she caught sight of me and took hold of my arm again and again, and implored me to look after Franz out there. Indeed he did have a face like a child, and such frail bones that after four weeks' pack-carrying he already had flat feet. But how can a man look after anyone in the field!

"Now you will soon be going home," says Kropp. "You would have had to wait at least three or four months for your leave."

Kemmerich nods. I cannot bear to look at his hands, they are like wax. Under the nails is the dirt of the trenches, it shows through blue-black like poison. It strikes me that these nails will continue to grow like lean fantastic cellar-plants long after Kemmerich breathes no more. I see the picture before me. They twist themselves into corkscrews and grow and grow, and with them the hair on the decaying skull, just like grass in a good soil, just like grass, how can it be possible—

Müller leans over. "We have brought your things, Franz."

Kemmerich signs with his hands. "Put them under the bed."

Müller does so. Kemmerich starts on again about the watch. How can one calm him without making him suspicious?

Müller reappears with a pair of airman's boots. They are fine English boots of soft, yellow leather which reach to the knees and lace up all the way—they are things to be coveted.

Müller is delighted at the sight of them. He matches their soles against his own clumsy boots and says: "Will you be taking them with you then, Franz?"

We all three have the same thought; even if he should get better, he would

be able to use only one—they are no use to him. But as things are now it is a pity that they should stay here; the orderlies will of course grab them as soon as he is dead.

"Won't you leave them with us?" Müller repeats.

Kemmerich doesn't want to. They are his most prized possessions.

"Well, we could exchange," suggests Müller again. "Out here one can make some use of them." Still Kemmerich is not to be moved.

I tread on Müller's foot; reluctantly he puts the fine boots back again under the bed.

We talk a little more and then take our leave.

"Cheerio, Franz."

I promise him to come back in the morning. Müller talks of doing so, too. He is thinking of the lace-up boots and means to be on the spot.

Kemmerich groans. He is feverish. We get hold of an orderly outside and ask him to give Kemmerich a dose of morphia.

He refuses. "If we were to give morphia to everyone we would have to have tubs full—"

"You only attend to officers properly," says Kropp viciously.

I hastily intervene and give him a cigarette. He takes it.

"Are you usually allowed to give it, then?" I ask him.

He is annoyed. "If you don't think so, then why do you ask?"

I press a few more cigarettes into his hand. "Do us the favour—"

"Well, all right," he says.

Kropp goes in with him. He doesn't trust him and wants to see. We wait outside.

Müller returns to the subject of the boots. "They would fit me perfectly. In these boots I get blister after blister. Do you think he will last till tomorrow after drill? If he passes out in the night, we know where the boots—"

Kropp returns. "Do you think—?" he asks.

"He's done for," says Müller emphatically.

We go back to the huts. I think of the letter that I must write tomorrow to Kemmerich's mother. I am freezing. I could do with a tot of rum. Müller pulls up some grass and chews it. Suddenly little Kropp throws his cigarette away, stamps on it savagely, and looking around him with a broken and distracted face, stammers "Damned shit, the damned shit!"

We walk on for a long time. Kropp has calmed himself; we understand, he saw red; out there every man gets like that sometime.

"What has Kantorek written to you?" Müller asks him.

He laughs. "We are the Iron Youth."

We all three smile bitterly, Kropp rails: he is glad that he can speak.

Yes, that's the way they think, these hundred thousand Kantoreks! Iron Youth! Youth! We are none of us more than twenty years old. But young? Youth? That is long ago. We are old folk.

What would you do if you were very ill but denied medical care? In this excerpt from the novel, Kino and his wife Juana are desperate when their baby Coyotito is bitten by a deadly scorpion. Read to find out what happens when this poor Indian family in Mexico asks a rich doctor for help.

The Pearl

John Steinbeck (1902–1968)

Kino awakened in the near dark. The stars still shone and the day had drawn only a pale wash of light in the lower sky to the east. The roosters had been crowing for some time, and the early pigs were already beginning their ceaseless turning of twigs and bits of wood to see whether anything to eat had been overlooked. Outside the brush house in the tuna clump, a covey of little birds chittered and flurried with their wings.

Kino's eyes opened, and he looked first at the lightening square which was the door and then he looked at the hanging box where Coyotito slept. And last he turned his head to Juana, his wife, who lay beside him on the mat, her blue head shawl over her nose and over her breasts and around the small of her back. Juana's eyes were open too. Kino could never remember seeing them closed when he awakened. Her dark eyes made little reflected stars. She was looking at him as she was always looking at him when he awakened.

Kino heard the little splash of morning waves on the beach. It was very good—Kino closed his eyes again to listen to his music. Perhaps he alone did this and perhaps all of his people did it. His people had once been great makers of songs so that everything

The Pearl   45

they saw or thought or did or heard became a song. That was very long ago. The songs remained; Kino knew them, but no new songs were added. That does not mean that there were no personal songs. In Kino's head there was a song now, clear and soft, and if he had been able to speak it, he would have called it the Song of the Family.

His blanket was over his nose to protect him from the dank air. His eyes flicked to a rustle beside him. It was Juana arising, almost soundlessly. On her hard bare feet she went to the hanging box where Coyotito slept, and she leaned over and said a little reassuring word. Coyotito looked up for a moment and closed his eyes and slept again.

Juana went to the fire pit and uncovered a coal and fanned it alive while she broke little pieces of brush over it.

Now Kino got up and wrapped his blanket about his head and nose and shoulders. He slipped his feet into his sandals and went outside to watch the dawn.

Outside the door he squatted down and gathered the blanket ends about his knees. He saw the specks of Gulf clouds flame high in the air. And a goat came near and sniffed at him and stared with its cold yellow eyes. Behind him Juana's fire leaped into flame and threw spears of light through the chinks of the brush-house wall and threw a wavering square of light out the door. A late moth blustered in to find the fire. The Song of the Family came now from behind Kino. And the

rhythm of the family song was the grinding stone where Juana worked the corn for the morning cakes.

The dawn came quickly now, a wash, a glow, a lightness, and then an explosion of fire as the sun arose out of the Gulf. Kino looked down to cover his eyes from the glare. He could hear the pat of the corncakes in the house and the rich smell of them on the cooking plate. The ants were busy on the ground, big black ones with shiny bodies, and little dusty quick ants. Kino watched with the detachment of God while a dusty ant frantically tried to escape the sand trap an ant lion had dug for him. A thin, timid dog came close and, at a soft word from Kino, curled up, arranged its tail neatly over its feet, and laid its chin delicately on the pile. It was a black dog with yellow-gold spots where its eyebrows should have been. It was a morning like other mornings and yet perfect among mornings.

Kino heard the creak of the rope when Juana took Coyotito out of his hanging box and cleaned him and hammocked him in her shawl in a loop that placed him close to her breast. Kino could see these things without looking at them. Juana sang softly an ancient song that had only three notes and yet endless variety of interval. And this was part of the family song too. It was all part. Sometimes it rose to an aching chord that caught the throat, saying this is safety, this is warmth, this is the *Whole*.

Across the brush fence were other brush houses, and the smoke came from them too, and the sound of breakfast, but those were other songs, their pigs were other pigs, their wives were not Juana. Kino was young and strong and his black hair hung over his brown forehead. His eyes were warm and fierce and bright and his mustache was thin and coarse. He lowered his blanket from his nose now, for the dark poisonous air was gone and the yellow sunlight fell on the house. Near the brush fence two roosters bowed and feinted at each other with squared wings and neck feathers ruffed out. It would be a clumsy fight. They were not game chickens. Kino watched them for a moment, and then his eyes went up to a flight of wild doves twinkling inland to the hills. The world was awake now, and Kino arose and went into his brush house.

As he came through the door Juana stood up from the glowing fire pit. She put Coyotito back in his hanging box and then she combed her black hair and braided it in two braids and tied the ends with thin green ribbon. Kino squatted by the fire pit and rolled a hot corncake and dipped it in sauce and ate it. And he drank a little pulque and that was breakfast. That was the only breakfast he had ever known outside of feast days and one incredible fiesta on cookies that had nearly killed him. When Kino had finished, Juana came back to the fire and ate her breakfast. They had spoken once, but there is not need for speech if it is only a habit anyway. Kino sighed with satisfaction— and that was conversation.

The sun was warming the brush house, breaking through its crevices in long streaks. And one of the streaks fell on the hanging box where Coyotito lay, and on the ropes that held it.

It was a tiny movement that drew their eyes to the hanging box. Kino and Juana froze in their positions. Down the rope that hung the baby's box from the roof support a scorpion moved slowly. His stinging tail was straight out behind him, but he could whip it up in a flash of time.

Kino's breath whistled in his nostrils and he opened his mouth to stop it. And then the startled look was gone from him and the rigidity from his body. In his mind a new song had

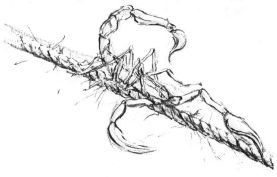

come, the Song of Evil, the music of the enemy, of any foe of the family, a savage, secret, dangerous melody, and underneath, the Song of the Family cried plaintively.

The scorpion moved delicately down the rope toward the box. Under her breath Juana repeated an ancient magic to guard against such evil, and on top of that she muttered a Hail Mary between clenched teeth. But Kino was in motion. His body glided quietly across the room, noiselessly and smoothly. His hands were in front of him, palms down, and his eyes were on the scorpion. Beneath it in the hanging box Coyotito laughed and reached up his hand toward it. It sensed danger when Kino was almost within reach of it. It stopped, and its tail rose up over its back in little jerks and the curved thorn on the tail's end glistened.

Kino stood perfectly still. He could hear Juana whispering the old magic again, and he could hear the evil music of the enemy. He could not move until the scorpion moved, and it felt for the source of the death that was coming to it. Kino's hand went forward very slowly, very smoothly. The thorned tail jerked upright. And at that moment the laughing Coyotito shook the rope and the scorpion fell.

Kino's hand leaped to catch it, but it fell past his fingers, fell on the baby's shoulder, landed and struck. Then, snarling, Kino had it, had it in his fingers, rubbing it to a paste in his hands. He threw it down and beat it into the earth floor with his fist, and Coyotito screamed with pain in his box. But Kino beat and stamped the enemy until it was only a fragment and a moist place in the dirt. His teeth were bared and fury flared in his eyes

and the Song of the Enemy roared in his ears.

But Juana had the baby in her arms now. She found the puncture with redness starting from it already. She put her lips down over the puncture and sucked hard and spat and sucked again while Coyotito screamed.

Kino hovered; he was helpless, he was in the way.

The screams of the baby brought the neighbors. Out of their brush houses they poured—Kino's brother Juan Tomás and his fat wife Apolonia and their four children crowded in the door and blocked the entrance, while behind them others tried to look in, and one small boy crawled among legs to have a look. And those in front passed the word back to those behind— "Scorpion. The baby has been stung."

Juana stopped sucking the puncture for a moment. The little hole was slightly enlarged and its edges whitened from the sucking, but the red swelling extended farther around it in a hard lymphatic mound. And all of these people knew about the scorpion. An adult might be very ill from the sting, but a baby could easily die from the poison. First, they knew, would come swelling and fever and tightened throat, and then cramps in the stomach, and then Coyotito might die if enough of the poison had gone in. But the stinging pain of the bite was going away. Coyotito's screams turned to moans.

Kino had wondered often at the iron in his patient, fragile wife. She, who was obedient and respectful and cheerful and patient, she could arch her back in child pain with hardly a cry. She could stand fatigue and hunger almost better than Kino himself. In the canoe she was like a strong man. And now she did a most surprising thing.

"The doctor," she said. "Go to get the doctor."

The word was passed out among the neighbors where they stood close packed in the little yard behind the brush fence. And they repeated among themselves, "Juana wants the doctor." A wonderful thing, a memorable thing, to want the doctor. To get him would be a remarkable thing. The doctor never came to the cluster of brush houses. Why should he, when he had more than he could do to take care of the rich people who lived in the stone and plaster houses of the town.

"He would not come," the people in the yard said.

"He would not come," the people in the door said, and the thought got into Kino.

"The doctor would not come," Kino said to Juana.

She looked up at him, her eyes as cold as the eyes of a lioness. This was Juana's first baby—this was nearly everything there was in Juana's world. And Kino saw her determination and the music of the family sounded in his head with a steely tone.

"Then we will go to him," Juana said, and with one hand she arranged her dark blue shawl over her head and made of one end of it a sling to hold the moaning baby and made of the other end of it a shade over his eyes to protect him from the light. The people in the door pushed against those behind to let her through. Kino followed her. They went out of the gate to the rutted path and the neighbors followed them.

The thing had become a neighborhood affair. They made a quick soft-footed procession into the center of the town, first Juana and Kino, and behind them Juan Tomás and Apolonia, her big stomach jiggling with the strenuous pace, then all the neighbors with the children trotting on the flanks. And the yellow sun threw their black shadows ahead of them so that they walked on their own shadows.

They came to the place where the brush houses stopped and the city of stone and plaster began, the city of harsh outer walls and inner cool gardens where a little water played and the bougainvillaea crusted the walls with purple and brick-red and white. They heard from the secret gardens the singing of caged birds and heard the splash of cooling water on hot flag-stones. The procession crossed the blinding plaza and passed in front of the church. It had grown now, and on the outskirts the hurrying newcomers were being softly informed how the baby had been stung by a scorpion, how the father and mother were taking it to the doctor.

And the newcomers, particularly the beggars from the front of the church who were great experts in financial analysis, looked quickly at Juana's old blue skirt, saw the tears in her shawl, appraised the green ribbon on her braids, read the age of Kino's blanket and the thousand washings of his clothes, and set them down as poverty people and went along to see what kind of drama might develop. The four beggars in front of the church knew everything in the town. They were students of the expressions of young women as they went into confession, and they saw them as they came out and read the nature of the sin. They knew every little scandal and some very big crimes. They slept at their posts in the shadow of the church so that no one crept in for consolation without their knowledge. And they knew the doctor. They knew his ignorance, his cruelty, his avarice,[1] his appetites, his sins. They knew his clumsy abortions and the little brown pennies he gave sparingly for alms. They had seen his corpses go into the church. And, since early Mass was over and business was slow, they followed the procession, these endless searchers after perfect knowledge of their fellow men, to see what the fat lazy doctor would do about an indigent[2] baby with a scorpion bite.

The scurrying procession came at last to the big gate in the wall of the doctor's house. They could hear the splashing water and the singing of caged birds and the sweep of the long brooms on the flagstones. And they could smell the frying of good bacon from the doctor's house.

Kino hesitated a moment. This doctor was not of his people. This doctor was of a race which for nearly

---

1. avarice: greed.
2. indigent: poor.

four hundred years had beaten and starved and robbed and despised Kino's race, and frightened it too, so that the indigene came humbly to the door. And as always when he came near to one of this race, Kino felt weak and afraid and angry at the same time. Rage and terror went together. He could kill the doctor more easily than he could talk to him, for all of the doctor's race spoke to all of Kino's race as though they were simple animals. And as Kino raised his right hand to the iron ring knocker in the gate, rage swelled in him, and the pounding music of the enemy beat in his ears, and his lips drew tight against his teeth— but with his left hand he reached to take off his hat. The iron ring pounded against the gate. Kino took off his hat and stood waiting. Coyotito moaned a little in Juana's arms and she spoke softly to him. The procession crowded close the better to see and hear.

After a moment the big gate opened a few inches. Kino could see the green coolness of the garden and little splashing fountain through the opening. The man who looked out at him was one of his own race. Kino spoke to him in the old language. "The little one—the first born—has been poisoned by the scorpion," Kino said. "He requires the skill of the healer."

The gate closed a little, and the servant refused to speak in the old language. "A little moment," he said. "I go to inform myself," and he closed the gate and slid the bolt home. The glaring sun threw the bunched shadows of the people blackly on the white wall.

In his chamber the doctor sat up in his high bed. He had on his dressing gown of red watered silk that had come from Paris, a little tight over the chest now if it was buttoned. On his lap was a silver tray with a silver chocolate pot and a tiny cup of eggshell china, so delicate that it looked silly when he lifted it with his big hand, lifted it with the tips of thumb and forefinger and spread the other three fingers wide to get them out of the way. His eyes rested in puffy little hammocks of flesh and his mouth drooped with discontent. He was growing very stout, and his voice was hoarse with the fat that pressed on his throat. Beside him on a table was a small Oriental gong and a bowl of cigarettes. The furnishings of the room were heavy and dark and gloomy. The pictures were religious, even the large tinted photograph of his dead wife, who, if Masses willed and paid for out of her own estate could do it, was in Heaven. The doctor had once for a short time been a part of the great world and his whole subsequent life was memory and longing for France. "That," he said, "was civilized living"— by which he meant that on a small income he had been able to keep a mistress and eat in restaurants. He poured his second cup of chocolate and crumbled a sweet biscuit in his fingers. The servant from the gate came to the open door and stood waiting to be noticed.

"Yes?" the doctor asked.

"It is a little Indian with a baby. He says a scorpion stung it."

The doctor put his cup down gently before he let his anger rise.

"Have I nothing better to do than cure insect bites for 'little Indians'? I am a doctor, not a veterinary."

"Yes, Patron," said the servant.

"Has he any money?" the doctor demanded. "No, they never have any money. I, I alone in the world am supposed to work for nothing—and I am tired of it. See if he has any money!"

At the gate the servant opened the door a trifle and looked out at the waiting people. And this time he spoke in the old language.

"Have you money to pay for the treatment?"

Now Kino reached into a secret place somewhere under his blanket. He brought out a paper folded many times. Crease by crease he unfolded it, until at last there came to view eight small misshapen seed pearls, as ugly and gray as little ulcers, flattened and almost valueless. The servant took the paper and closed the gate again, but this time he was not gone long. He opened the gate just wide enough to pass the paper back.

"The doctor has gone out," he said. "He was called to a serious case." And he shut the gate quickly out of shame.

And now a wave of shame went over the whole procession. They melted away. The beggars went back to the church steps, the stragglers moved off, and the neighbors departed so that the public shaming of Kino would not be in their eyes.

For a long time Kino stood in front of the gate with Juana beside him. Slowly he put his suppliant hat on his head. Then, without warning, he struck the gate a crushing blow with his fist. He looked down in wonder at his split knuckles and at the blood that flowed down between his fingers.

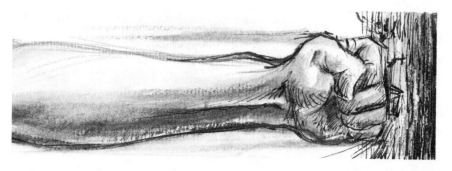

Unit 3: Nonfiction

Literature is the art of writing
something that will be read twice.
                                    Cyril Connolly

More and more readers are enjoying the rewards of reading nonfiction. Nonfiction is literature about actual people and events. As you are about to discover, it offers a view of real life that is both fascinating and reassuring.

If you have ever had trouble communicating with a child, Erma Bombeck, the author of the first selection, will reassure you that you are not alone. You'll be entertained by her amusing accounts of life in the Bombeck household.

The next selection is a commentary on television commercials. The author's skillful blend of facts and opinions may persuade you to his point of view that some commercials are powerful indeed. Read to decide if you agree.

The remaining selections in this nonfiction unit deal with the lives of two memorable people. One young man named Thoreau will take you into the quiet woods outside of Concord, Massachusetts, as he observes nature and reflects on life. Jane Addams will involve you in her attempts to improve life in a poor Chicago neighborhood. Both selections offer a glimpse of America in the 1800s.

Read to discover why so many people enjoy this special kind of literature called nonfiction.

Do children have a language of their own? In this excerpt from the book **If Life Is a Bowl of Cherries, What Am I Doing in the Pits?**, *the author Erma Bombeck comments humorously on everyday family life. Read about one mother's comical attempt to understand her children.*

How to Speak Child Fluently

Erma Bombeck (1927–1996)

I will never understand children. I never pretended to. I meet mothers all the time who make resolutions to themselves. "I'm going to develop patience with my children and go out of my way to show them I am interested in them and what they do. I am going to understand my children." These women wind up making rag rugs, using blunt scissors.

I firmly believe kids don't want your understanding. They want your trust, your compassion, your blinding love and your car keys, but you try to understand them and you're in big trouble. To me, they remain life's greatest mysteries.

I have never understood, for example, how come a child can climb up on the roof, scale the TV antenna and rescue the cat—yet cannot walk down the hallway without grabbing both walls with his grubby hands for balance.

Or how come a child can eat yellow snow, kiss the dog on the lips, chew gum that he found in the ashtray, put his mouth over a muddy garden hose... and refuse to drink from a glass his brother has just used.

Why is it he can stand with one foot on first base while reaching out and plucking a baseball off the ground with the tips of his fingers...yet cannot pick up a piece of soap before it melts into the drain.

I've seen kids ride bicycles, run, play ball, set up a camp, swing, fight a war, swim and race for eight hours, . . . yet have to be driven to the garbage can.

It puzzles me how a child can see a dairy bar three miles away, but cannot see a 4 x 6 rug that has scrunched up under his feet and has been dragged through two rooms. Maybe you know why a child can reject a hot dog with mustard served on a soft bun at home, yet eat six of them two hours later at fifty cents each.

Did you ever wonder how you can trip over a kid's shoes under the kitchen sink, in the bathroom, on the front porch, under the coffee table, in the sandbox, in the car, in the clothes hamper and on the washer . . . but can never find them when it is time to cut grass?

If child raising were to be summed up in one word, it's frustration. You think you're on the inside track and you find you're still in the starting gate. It's not that you expect dividends for what you're doing . . . only a few meager returns.

Okay, take the car incident. My oldest took her car to the garage for repairs last week and used my car while hers was being fixed.

For three days I sat home without wheels (which is like telling Zsa Zsa Gabor she can't have any more wedding cake).

On the day her car came back she returned my car keys and said, "Hey Mom, you owe me three dollars for the gas I put in your car."

I could not believe what she was saying. These words were being uttered by a child I poured eight hundred and eighty-seven dollars' worth of vitamins down. Paid one hundred fifty-four dollars for her old teeth under the pillow. Indulged in two thousand dollars' worth of toys (batteries extra). Footed the bill for one hundred eighty-six skin preparations to kill a single pimple. Sent to camp. Took the sink apart to find her lost class ring. Worried myself sick when she cracked an A in human sexuality.

Then I remembered a letter that a teenager had written me after she had read one of my books. Maybe that would get through to her.

"Listen to this," I said, reading from the letter.

"*Parents go through life, Mrs. Bombeck, saying to their children, 'I've worked my fingers to the bone for you. I've made sacrifices and what do I get in return?'*

"*You want an answer, Mrs. Bombeck? You get messy rooms, filthy clothing, disheveled hair, dirty fingernails, raided refrigerators ad nauseam. You get something else too. You get someone who loves you but never takes the time to tell you in words. You get someone who'll defend you at every turn even though you do wear orthopedic socks and enjoy listening to Pat Boone and changing your underwear everyday and acknowledging their presence in public.*

"*Yes, sometimes you talked too much and sometimes you turned away too soon. But you laughed with us and cried with us and all the agony, non-communication, frustrations, fears and*

WOMEN DREAMING OF ESCAPE, 1945, Joan Miro, Mr. and Mrs. Morton Neumann Collection, Chicago, copyright 1990 ARS N.Y./ADAGP

angers showed us that despite the need to be free and independent and do our own thing...you cared.

"And when we leave home, there will be a little tug at our hearts because we know we will miss you and home and everything it meant. But most of all, we will miss the constantly assured knowledge of how very much you love us."

My daughter looked up. Her eyes were misty. "Does that mean I don't get the three bucks?"

In a way, I blame experts for the mess parents are in today. They laid a ton of guilt on us so that we questioned every move we made.

I read one psychologist's theory that said, "Never strike a child in anger." When could I strike him? When he is kissing me on my birthday? When he is recuperating from measles? Do I slap the Bible out of his hand on Sunday?

Another expert said, "Be careful in the way you discipline your children or you could permanently damage their Id."

Damage it! I didn't even know where it was. For all I knew it either made you sterile or caused dandruff. Once I suspected where it was, I made the kid wear four diapers just to be safe.

And scratch the wonderful "pal" theory that worked so great with our parents. My son slouched into the kitchen one night, threw his books on the countertop and said, "I've just had the worst day of my entire life and it's all your fault."

"How do you figure that?" I asked.

"Just because you made me go back up to my room and turn off all the lights before I went to school, I missed the bus. Then, with all your nagging about cleaning up my room, I couldn't find my gym clothes and got fifteen points knocked off my grade."

"The gym clothes were folded in your bottom drawer."

"Yeah, well, what yo-yo would expect them to be there?"

"You've got a point."

"I hope you're happy," he grumbled. "I have failed English."

"I did that?"

"That's right. I told you I had a paper that was due before lunch and you made me turn off my lights last night and wouldn't let me do it."

"It was one-thirty in the morning."

"Just forget it. It's done. Did you have a good lunch today? I hope so because, thanks to you, I didn't get any."

"What's THAT got to do with me?"

"You're the one who wouldn't advance me next week's allowance. And more good news. You know the suede jacket you got me for my birthday last year? Well, it's gone."

"And I'm to blame for that?"

"I'm glad you admit it. All I hear around here is, 'Hang up your coat, hang up your pajamas, hang up your sweater...' and the one time I take your advice and hang up my jacket on a hook in the lunchroom, someone rips it off. If I had just dropped it on the floor by my feet like I always do, I'd have that suede jacket today."

"It sounds like quite a day."

"It's not over yet," he said. "Didn't you forget something?"

"Like what?" I asked.

"Like, weren't you supposed to remind me I had ball practice after school?"

"I put a note on your desk."

"Under all that junk I'm supposed to find a note! It would serve you right if I got cut. And I might just do that. I swear, I was talking to some of the guys and we decided parents can sure screw up their kids."

I smiled. "We try."

In analyzing the problem of parenting and understanding children, it would seem inevitable that this country will eventually resort to a Parental Park 'N' Swap.

I have never met a child who did not feel that he is maligned, harassed and overworked and would do better if he had Mrs. Jones for a mother who loves untidiness and eats out a lot.

On the other hand, I have never met a parent who did not feel unappreciated, persecuted, servile and would have been better off with Rodney Phipps who doesn't talk with food in his mouth and bought his mother a hair dryer for Mother's Day.

What I'm suggesting is a Sears parking lot that could be made available every Saturday afternoon, where parents and their offspring could come to look, compare and eventually swap if they felt they could do better.

When I mentioned this to my card club, they fairly quivered with excitement. "I have always wanted to 'trade up' to a child who picked towels up off the floor," said Peg.

How to Speak Child Fluently

"I have one like that," said Dorothy. "But she's a drain stuffer. If it doesn't fit down the drain she lifts out the trap and shoves it down."

"That doesn't sound so bad," said Evelyn. "I'd take a drain stuffer over a shower freak anyday. Empties a forty-gallon water tank three times a day."

"At least she's clean," said June. "I'll swap someone a long-hair who is an endangered species. Someday he's going to get lost behind that hair and never find his way out again."

"LOOK," said Peg, "I'm going to make you an offer you can't refuse. I'll offer my towel dropper for a boy who never learned how to use the telephone and I'll throw in a three weeks' supply of clean underwear."

"I'll do you one better," I said. "I'll swap or trade a quiet boy who is never late to dinner, gets up when he is called, sits up straight, has just finished two years with his orthodontist, is reasonable to operate and doesn't play his stereo too loud. No offer is too ridiculous."

The entire card table put down their cards and leaned forward. Finally June asked, "What's the catch?"

"No catch. He just knows two words...'You know?'."

Everyone went home keeping what they had and feeling better about it.

When does parenting end?

It all depends on how you regard your children. Do you see them as an appliance that is under warranty to perform and when they start to cost money, get rid of them?

Are they like an endowment policy you invest in for eighteen or twenty years and then they return dividends through your declining years?

Or are they like a finely gilded mirror that reflects the owner in every way and one day when you see a flaw in it, a distortion or one tiny idea that is different from your own, you cast it out and declare yourself a failure?

I said to my husband one night, "I see our children as kites. You spend a lifetime trying to get them off the ground. You run with them until you're both breathless...they crash...you add a longer tail...they hit the roof-top...you pluck them out of the spouting...you patch and comfort, adjust and teach. You watch them lifted by the wind and assure them that someday they'll fly...Finally, they're airborne, but they need more string and with each twist of the ball of twine, there is a sadness that goes with the joy because the kite becomes more distant and somehow you know it won't be long before this beautiful creature will snap the lifeline binding you together and soar as it was meant to soar—free and alone."

"That was beautiful," said my husband. "Are you finished?"

"I think so. Why?"

"Because one of your kites just crashed into the garage door with his car...another is landing here with three surfboards with friends on them and the third is hung up at college and needs more string to come home for the holidays."

Do people really watch television commercials? Like it or not, some commercials have a way of grabbing a viewer's attention. Read this commentary to find out how ad makers create such commercials.

Why You Watch Some Commercials— Whether You Mean to or Not

David H. Friedman (1949–   )

Zap! Zip! Flip!

No, Batman isn't back. These are the sounds of television advertisers taking it on the chin from consumer technology. More and more viewers are reaching for remote controls to switch channels ("zap!" and "flip!") and to fast-forward through VCR tapes ("zip!")—all to avoid commercials.

Advertisers aren't about to take this lying down. Desperate to keep you tuned in to their pitches, they're trying some new tricks. If that's news to you, it may be because these new techniques are manipulating you in ways you're not aware of. "Many of these commercials have more impact on the subconscious level," charges New York University media professor Neil Postman. Perhaps more disturbing, ad agencies often enlist psychologists and neurophysiologists to make sure the pitches have the desired effect.

There are many examples of high-tech, hard-to-resist commercials.

Not-quite-seeing is believing.

Commercials may have been boring or irritating in the old days, but at least you could count on steady camera work and a clear message. Today, many advertisers are out to confuse you and throw you off balance with film footage that wouldn't pass muster with a junior-high film club. You have to stare at the screen just to figure out what's going on—and that, of course, is part of the idea.

Take the ads for Wang computers. In these hazy, washed-out spots, people walk partially in and out of the camera frame talking in computer jargon. But the confusion grabs attention, insists Jack Sansolo, vice-chairman of Hill, Holliday, Connors, Cosmopulos, the Boston ad agency that produced the spots. "The eavesdropping camera provides layers of meaning," he says. "Even people who don't understand a word of it are riveted to the screen."

The new ad campaign for Nissan cars uses the badder-is-better approach to inject a note of sincerity. The grainy, shaky scenes look like something out of a home movie, and that makes the ad seem more honest, says Lee Clow, president of Nissan's ad agency, Chiat/Day in Los Angeles. "Honesty is in right now," he notes.

Remember subliminal ads? Back in the early '60s, some experts warned that advertisers could flash messages on the screen so quickly that the messages would subconsciously get through without viewers realizing they had seen anything. No, advertisers aren't trying that now. But some are trying the next best thing: images flashed so quickly you barely have a chance to register them.

"Sudden changes in scene cause an involuntary increase in brain activity," explains Michael Rothschild, an associate professor of marketing at the University of Wisconsin who works

with the advertising industry. Rothschild has been wiring commercial-watchers up to devices that measure brain function. He's found that the ability to remember a commercial seems to increase with brain activity at viewing time.

Pontiac has capitalized on this phenomenon with its most recent ads, in which a long shot is one and one-half seconds, and the shortest shots flash by in one-quarter of a second. Noel Nauber, group creative director at D'Arcy Masius Benton & Bowles in Bloomfield Hills, Mich., who created the spot, says the commercial scored much higher than average among test audiences asked to recall the spot.

Not even children are spared from the rapid-fire technique. In fact, they may have it worse. Hill, Holliday, for example, employs machine-gun editing in its new ads for VideoArt, a sort of electronic paint brush for children. "Kids are barraged with images and speed these days—how else are you going to break through?" asks Hill, Holliday's Sansolo.

Whine, beep, hum.
Dr. William Winn is a Boston psychologist who has become increasingly concerned about the new

advertising techniques. "We need to be increasingly vigilant[1] about recognizing the ways we're being manipulated as the advertising industry gets more technically sophisticated," he warns. "They're paid to sell you on a product whether it's good for you or not, and every year they're becoming more competent at it."

This competence goes beyond assaulting you visually; advertisers are going after your ears as well. Neurophysiologist Eric Courchesne of the University of California at San Diego Medical School has been observing the powerful effects certain sounds have on human brain waves. His work isn't news to admakers, he insists. "Advertisers are using sounds to take advantage of the automatic systems built into the brain that force you to stop what you're doing and refocus on the screen," he explains. "You can't ignore these sounds." That's why commercials are starting off with noises ranging from a baby crying (Advil) to a car horn (Hertz) to a factory whistle (Almond Joy).

"We know from research that a sound change makes you look toward the screen," says Ron Milavsky, a sociologist who is vice president of social research at NBC. He adds that NBC's recent promo for Tom Brokaw was successful largely because it started off with a forceful voice-over saying "Washington" and then pausing before continuing with a list of geographical hot spots.

In seeking the right sound, advertisers will use whatever works to pull you into the commercial—even if

the noises are less than pleasant. New York ad agency McCann-Erickson Worldwide added a penetrating electronic hum to its stark, white-type-on-black-screen visuals for Shearson Lehman Brothers, an investment firm. The hum "is an audio presence that supports the seriousness of the message," says Bruce Nelson, who helped develop the ad.

Advertisers can even be downright merciless in their choice of sound. Ads for pain reliever Nuprin kick off by assaulting viewers with the whine of a dentist's drill, complete with a powerful flash of light from a dentist's examining light. Explains Harry Azorin, vice president and group creative director with Grey Advertising: "We wanted to help the viewer recall a type of pain that we've all experienced." Hey, thanks.

In comparison, we should be sincerely grateful to Leo Burnett Company in Chicago. The agency went with an opera aria to pull viewers into a wordless demonstration of Cheer detergent cleaning a handkerchief in an ice-filled cocktail shaker. Then again, less highly cultured viewers might prefer the dentist's drill.

Feeling bad is good.

Advertisers have long known that commercials that make you feel good are likely to make you feel good about the product. But more recent research indicates that advertisers might be able to do even better with ads that evoke unpleasant feelings. If getting you to

---

1. **vigilant:** watchful; alert to danger.

suffer will boost sales, don't expect advertisers to shrink from the task.

Even AT&T, the king of the warm fuzzies, is moving to commercials designed to make you feel lousy. In commercials for the company's business phones a hyperactive camera ricochets around the face and hands of a person reciting a woeful tale of a phone-system breakdown. "One of our intentions was to make people feel anxiety," explains William Higgins, AT&T's manager of business advertising. For good measure, John Doig, creative director at AT&T's ad agency Ogilvy & Mather in New York, electronically took out much of the color "to accentuate the feeling of nervousness."

Advertisers have no shortage of ways to play on unpleasant thoughts. Volkswagen effectively employs fear in recent spots that show VWs hurtling down a test track at supremely confident VW engineers. (Or maybe they're not so confident; the ad employs stuntpeople instead of real VW engineers.)

How do advertisers know if their emotional manipulations are getting through? Psychologists and neurophysiologists have designed a dizzying array of procedures to measure the responses of test audiences. Volkswagen had viewers press buttons on a sort of emotion meter while they watched various ads. For the scary test-track commercials, "the needle went right off the scale," notes Volkswagen U.S.'s vice president, Jim Fuller. Some agencies turn to advertising research firms like NeuroCommunication Research Laboratories in Danbury, Conn., which measures the responses of viewers via sensors placed on their scalps. Others simply provide psychological questionnaires. One question Pontiac asked of its test viewers: "Did this commercial make you feel rather than think?" Most said yes, to Pontiac's delight.

Follow the swinging Fiero.

As if all this isn't enough, would you believe commercials might be hypnotizing you? Some experts maintain it's a possibility. "There is no question that hypnotic techniques are being used in certain commercials, whether knowingly or not," says Elliot Wineburg, a psychiatrist and assistant clinical professor at New York's Mount Sinai School of Medicine.

Wineburg—an ex-ad-copywriter who employs hypnosis in his treatment of stress-related illnesses—lists rapid scene changes, repetitive phrases, pulsating music and a recurring flashing of logos among the advertising techniques that can start to bring a viewer under. Among his nominations for Most Likely to Induce a Mild Trance: the Pontiac spot, a new Mercedes-Benz ad ("They keep flashing that star.") and the more high-energy entries from Coca-Cola and Pepsi. Wineburg notes that only about one out of four adults is highly susceptible to hypnosis. So relax—you might have bought that Mercedes for entirely different reasons.

The ad industry downplays the significance of its new techniques. "Psychological phenomena may come into play, but I wouldn't base a campaign on them," says Hill, Holliday's Sansolo. But critics disagree, insisting that some of the new techniques are being unfairly employed to get past viewers' defenses—and some insist such ads can cause real harm.

These critics are especially angered when advertisers aim the techniques at children. A number of children's interest groups were recently up in arms, for example, over a frightening and confusing ad (no longer aired) for Mattel's Captain Power in which young viewers were implored to use the toy to save the earth. "You don't need a psychologist to tell you that's sick," says Peggy Charren, president of Action for Children's Television in Cambridge, Mass.

As for the possibility of doing harm, New York University's Postman points to some beer commercials, which he says employ all the right techniques to reinforce some bad ideas. He contends, for example, that the quick cutting, exciting music and flashy imagery of "The Night Belongs to Michelob" campaign subconsciously provides a glamorous view of city night life—along with a few shots that subtly suggest driving is a part of it. "You get a wild, reckless sense from the pace," he says. (A Michelob spokesman denies that the ad promotes drinking and driving.)

What can we as viewers do about the way commercials affect us? Psychologist Winn suggests that parents ask their children—and each other—to pick out the commercials that most influence them and figure out why. "People discuss politics and school," he says. "Why not advertising?"

If the advertising industry gets any better at employing subtle psychological strategies, however, it may become nearly impossible to figure out the ways in which commercials are hitting home. That may be a little frightening, but it's not illegal—so don't expect the government to protect you from high-tech advertising, at least not in today's climate of deregulation. In the end, it's strictly viewer beware.

Have you ever wanted to live a simpler life? Thoreau, an American writer and philosopher, lived for two years in a small cabin on the shores of Walden Pond in Massachusetts. There he studied nature and thought deeply about life. He wanted to prove that people could live simply and be fully satisfied. Life today is different in many ways from life in 1845 when Thoreau wrote **Walden**. *Read these excerpts to find out if you think his ideas are still meaningful.*

From

Walden

Henry David Thoreau (1817–1862)

from Where I Lived, and What I Lived For

I went to the woods because I wished to live deliberately, to front only the essential facts of life, and see if I could not learn what it had to teach, and not, when I came to die, discover that I had not lived. I did not wish to live what was not life, living is so dear; nor did I wish to practice resignation, unless it was quite necessary. I wanted to live deep and suck out all the marrow of life, to live so sturdily and Spartan-like[1] as to put to rout all that was not life, to cut a broad swath and shave close, to drive life into a corner, and reduce it to its lowest terms, and, if it proved to be mean, why then to get the whole and genuine meanness of it, and publish its meanness to the world; or if it were sublime,[2] to know it by experience, and be able to give a true account of it in my next excursion. For most men, it appears to me, are in a strange uncertainty about it, whether it is of the devil or of God, and have *somewhat hastily* concluded that it is the chief end of man here to "glorify God and enjoy him forever."

Still we live meanly, like ants. Our life is frittered away by detail. An honest man has hardly need to count

1. **Spartan-like:** simply and with great self-discipline.
2. **sublime:** splendid.

POND PASS, 1974, Neil Welliver, Marlborough Galleries, New York

more than his ten fingers, or in extreme cases he may add his ten toes, and lump the rest. Simplicity, simplicity, simplicity! I say, let your affairs be as two or three, and not a hundred or a thousand; instead of a million count half a dozen, and keep your accounts on your thumbnail. Simplify, simplify. Instead of three meals a day, if it be necessary eat but one; instead of a hundred dishes, five; and reduce other things in proportion.

Let us spend one day as deliberately as Nature, and not be thrown off the track by every nutshell and mosquito's wing that falls on the rails. Let us rise early and fast, or break fast, gently and without perturbation;[3] let company come and let company go, let the bells ring and the children cry,— determined to make a day of it. Why should we knock under and go with the stream?

Time is but the stream I go a-fishing in. I drink at it; but while I drink I see the sandy bottom and detect how shallow it is. Its thin current slides away, but eternity remains. I would drink deeper; fish in the sky, whose bottom is pebbly with stars. I cannot count one. I know not the first letter of the alphabet, I have always been regretting that I was not as wise as the day I was born. The intellect is a cleaver;[4] it discerns and rifts its way into the secret of things. I do not wish

3. **perturbation:** disturbance.
4. **cleaver:** chopping tool.

to be any more busy with my hands than is necessary. My head is hands and feet. I feel all my best faculties concentrated in it. My instinct tells me that my head is an organ for burrowing, as some creatures use their snout and fore-paws, and with it I would mine and burrow my way through these hills. I think that the richest vein is somewhere hereabouts; so by the divining rod[5] and thin rising vapors I judge; and here I will begin to mine.

from **Solitude**

This is a delicious evening, when the whole body is one sense, and imbibes delight through every pore. I go and come with a strange liberty in Nature, a part of herself. As I walk along the stony shore of the pond in my shirt sleeves, though it is cool as well as cloudy and windy, and I see nothing special to attract me, all the elements are unusually congenial to me. The bullfrogs trump to usher in the night, and the note of the whippoorwill is borne on the rippling wind from over the water. Sympathy with the fluttering alder and poplar leaves almost takes away my breath; yet, like the lake, my serenity is rippled but not ruffled. These small waves raised by the evening wind are as remote from storm as the smooth reflecting surface. Though it is now dark, the wind still blows and roars in the wood, the waves still dash, and some creatures lull the rest with their notes. The repose is never complete. The wildest animals do not repose, but seek their prey now; the fox, and skunk, and rabbit, now

roam the fields and woods without fear. They are Nature's watchmen— links which connect the days of animated life.

When I return to my house I find that visitors have been there and left their cards, either a bunch of flowers, or a wreath of evergreen, or a name in pencil on a yellow walnut leaf or a chip. They who come rarely to the woods take some little piece of the forest into their hands to play with by the way, which they leave, either intentionally or accidentally. One has peeled a willow wand, woven it into a ring, and dropped it on my table. I could always tell if visitors had called in my absence, either by the bended twigs or grass, or the print of their shoes, and generally of what sex or age or quality they were by some slight trace left, as a flower dropped, or a bunch of grass plucked and thrown away, even as far off as the railroad, half a mile distant, or by the lingering odor of a cigar or pipe. Nay, I was frequently notified of the passage of a traveler along the highway sixty rods off by the scent of his pipe.

Men frequently say to me, "I should think you would feel lonesome down there, and want to be nearer to folks, rainy and snowy days and nights especially." I am tempted to reply to such, This whole earth which we inhabit is but a point in space. How far apart, think you, dwell the two most distant inhabitants of yonder star, the breadth of whose disk cannot be appreciated by our instruments? Why should I feel lonely? Is not our planet in

---

5. divining rod: rod used for finding water.

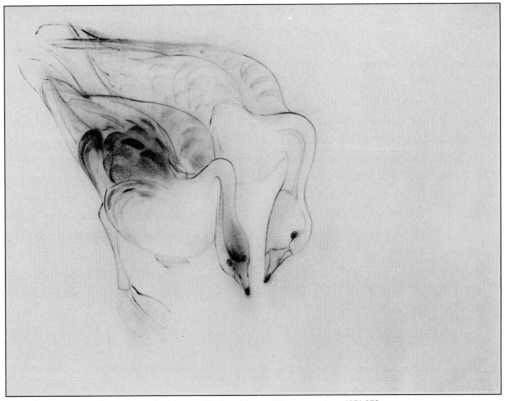

GANDERS, 1955, Morris Graves, Joslyn Art Museum, Omaha, Nebraska, Museum purchase 1971.272

the Milky Way? This which you put seems to me not to be the most important question. What sort of space is that which separates a man from his fellows and makes him solitary? I have found that no exertion of the legs can bring two minds much nearer to one another.

I find it wholesome to be alone the greater part of the time. To be in company, even with the best, is soon wearisome and dissipating. I love to be alone. I never found the companion that was so companionable as solitude. We are for the most part more lonely when we go abroad among men than when we stay in our chambers. A man thinking or working is always alone, let him be where he will. Solitude is not measured by the miles of space that intervene between a man and his fellows.

from Conclusion

I left the woods for as good a reason as I went there. Perhaps it seemed to me that I had several more lives to live, and could not spare any more time for that one. It is remarkable how easily and insensibly we fall into a particular route, and make a beaten track for ourselves. I had not lived there a week before my feet wore a path from my door to the pond-side; and though it is five or six years since I trod it, it is still quite distinct. It is true, I fear that others may have fallen into it, and so helped to keep it open. The surface of the earth is soft and impressible by the feet of men; and so with the paths which the mind travels. How worn and dusty, then, must be the highways of the world, how deep the ruts of tradition and conformity! I did not wish to take a cabin passage, but rather to go before the mast and on the deck of the world, for there I could best see the moonlight amid the mountains. I do not wish to go below now.

I learned this, at least, by my experiment: that if one advances confidently in the direction of his dreams, and endeavors to live the life which he has imagined, he will meet with a success unexpected in common hours. He will put some things behind, will pass an invisible boundary; new, universal, and more liberal laws will begin to establish themselves around and within him; or the old laws be expanded, and interpreted in his favor in a more liberal sense, and he will live with the license of a higher order of beings. In proportion as he simplifies his life, the laws of the universe will appear less complex, and solitude will not be solitude, nor poverty poverty, nor weakness weakness. If you have built castles in the air, your work need not be lost; that is where they should be. Now put the foundations under them.

Has anyone ever told you that your ideas were foolish and impractical? Some people thought Jane Addams, the author of this autobiographical excerpt, was foolish when she opened a settlement house in Chicago in 1889. But Miss Addams wanted to help the less fortunate people of the neighborhood. Read to find out about the social and educational services provided at Hull-House.

From

Twenty Years at Hull-House

Jane Addams (1860–1935)

The next January found Miss Starr and myself in Chicago, searching for a neighborhood in which we might put our plans into execution. . . .

In our search for a vicinity in which to settle we went about with the officers of the compulsory education department, with city missionaries and with the newspaper reporters whom I recall as a much older set of men than one ordinarily associates with that profession, or perhaps I was only sent out with the older ones on what they must all have considered a quixotic[1] mission. . . .

Three weeks later, with the advice of several of the oldest residents of Chicago, including the ex-mayor of the city, Colonel Mason, who had from the first been a warm friend to our plans, we decided upon a location somewhere near the junction of Blue Island Avenue, Halsted Street, and Harrison Street. I was surprised and overjoyed on the very first day of our search for quarters to come upon the hospitable old house, the quest for which I had so recently abandoned. The house was of course rented, the lower part of it used for offices and storerooms in connection with a factory that stood back of it. However, after some difficulties were overcome, it proved to be possible

---
1. **quixotic:** foolishly impractical.

to sublet the second floor and what had been the large drawing-room on the first floor.

The house had passed through many changes since it had been built in 1856 for the homestead of one of Chicago's pioneer citizens, Mr. Charles J. Hull, and although battered by its vicissitudes,[2] was essentially sound. Before it had been occupied by the factory, it had sheltered a second-hand furniture store, and at one time the Little Sisters of the Poor had used it for a home for the aged. It had a half-skeptical reputation for a haunted attic, so far respected by the tenants living on the second floor that they always kept a large pitcher full of water on the attic stairs. Their explanation of this custom was so incoherent that I was sure it was a survival of the belief that a ghost could not cross running water, but perhaps that interpretation was only my eagerness for finding folklore.

The fine old house responded kindly to repairs, its wide hall and open fireplaces always insuring it a gracious aspect. Its generous owner, Miss Helen Culver, in the following spring gave us a free leasehold of the entire house. Her kindness has continued through the years until the group of thirteen buildings, which at present comprises our equipment, is built largely upon land which Miss Culver has put at the service of the Settlement which bears Mr. Hull's name. . . .

We furnished the house as we would have furnished it were it in another part of the city, with the photographs and other impedimenta we had collected in Europe, and with a few bits of family mahogany. While all the new furniture which was bought was enduring in quality, we were careful to keep it in character with the fine old residence. Probably no young matron ever placed her own things in her own house with more pleasure than that with which we first furnished Hull-House. We believed that the Settlement may logically bring to its aid all those adjuncts which the cultivated man regards as good and suggestive of the best life of the past.

On the 18th of September, 1889, Miss Starr and I moved into it, with Miss Mary Keyser, who began by performing the housework, but who quickly developed into a very important factor in the life of the vicinity as well as in that of the household, and whose death five years later was most sincerely mourned by hundreds of our neighbors. In our enthusiasm over "settling," the first night we forgot not only to lock but to close a side door opening on Polk Street, and were much pleased in the morning to find that we possessed a fine illustration of the honesty and kindliness of our new neighbors.

Our first guest was an interesting young woman who lived in a neighboring tenement, whose widowed mother aided her in the support of the family by scrubbing a downtown theater every night. The mother, of English birth, was well bred and carefully educated, but was in the midst of that bitter struggle which

---

2. **vicissitudes**: natural changes.

awaits so many strangers in American cities who find that their social position tends to be measured solely by the standards of living they are able to maintain. Our guest has long since married the struggling young lawyer to whom she was then engaged, and he is now leading his profession in an eastern city. She recalls that month's experience always with a sense of amusement over the fact that the succession of visitors who came to see the new Settlement invariably questioned her most minutely concerning "these people" without once suspecting that they were talking to one who had been identified with the neighborhood from childhood. I at least was able to draw a lesson from the incident, and I never addressed a Chicago audience on the subject of the Settlement and its vicinity without inviting a neighbor to go with me, that I might curb any hasty generalization by the consciousness that I had an auditor who knew the conditions more intimately than I could hope to do. . . .

Volunteers to the new undertaking came quickly; a charming young girl conducted a kindergarten in the drawing-room, coming regularly every morning from her home in a distant part of the North Side of the city. . . .

That first kindergarten was a constant source of education to us. We were much surprised to find social distinctions even among its lambs, although greatly amused with the neat formulation made by the superior little Italian boy who refused to sit beside uncouth little Angelina because "we

Hull-House as it appeared in 1905.

AP/Wide World Photos

eat our macaroni this way,"—imitating the movement of a fork from a plate to his mouth,—"and she eat her macaroni this way," holding his hand high in the air and throwing back his head, that his wide-open mouth might receive an imaginary cascade. Angelina gravely nodded her little head in approval of this distinction between gentry[3] and peasant. "But isn't it astonishing that merely table manners are made such a test all the way along?" was the comment of their democratic teacher. . . .

The dozens of younger children who from the first came to Hull-House were organized into groups which were not quite classes and not quite clubs. The value of these groups consisted

3. gentry: the upper class.

almost entirely in arousing a higher imagination and in giving the children the opportunity which they could not have in the crowded schools, for initiative and for independent social relationships. The public schools then contained little handwork of any sort, so that naturally any instruction which we provided for the children took the direction of this supplementary work. But it required a constant effort that the pressure of poverty itself should not defeat the educational aim. The Italian girls in the sewing classes would count that day lost when they could not carry home a garment, and the insistence that it should be neatly made seemed a super-refinement to those in dire need of clothing.

As these clubs have been continued during the twenty years they have developed classes in the many forms of handicraft which the newer education is so rapidly adapting for the delight of children; but they still keep their essentially social character and still minister to that large number of children who leave school the very week they are fourteen years old, only too eager to close the schoolroom door forever on a tiresome task that is at last well over. It seems to us important that these children shall find themselves permanently attached to a House that offers them evening clubs and classes with their old companions, that merges as easily as possible the school life into the working life and does what it can to find places for the bewildered young things looking for work. A large proportion of the delinquent boys brought into the juvenile court in

1914 photograph of Jane Addams, 25 years after she opened Hull-House.

Chicago are the oldest sons in large families whose wages are needed at home. The grades from which many of them leave school, as the records show, are piteously far from the seventh and eighth where the very first instruction in manual training is given, nor have they been caught by any other abiding interest.

In spite of these flourishing clubs for children early established at Hull-House, and the fact that our first organized undertaking was a kindergarten, we were very insistent that the Settlement should not be primarily for the children, and that it was absurd to suppose that grown people would not respond to opportunities for education and social life. Our enthusiastic kindergartner herself demonstrated this with an old woman of ninety, who, because she was left alone all day while her daughter cooked in a restaurant, had formed such a persistent habit of picking the plaster off the walls that one landlord after another refused to have her for a tenant. It required but a few weeks' time to teach her to make large paper chains, and gradually she was content to do it all day long, and in the end took quite as much pleasure in adorning the walls as she had formerly taken in demolishing them. Fortunately the landlord had never heard the aesthetic principle that the exposure of basic construction is more desirable than gaudy decoration. In course of time it was discovered that the old woman could speak Gaelic, and when one or two grave professors came to see her, the neighborhood was filled with pride that such a wonder lived in their midst. To mitigate[4] life for a woman of ninety was an unfailing refutation[5] of the statement that the Settlement was designed for the young. . . .

In those early days we were often asked why we had come to live on Halsted Street when we could afford to live somewhere else. I remember one man who used to shake his head and say it was "the strangest thing he had met in his experience," but who was finally convinced that it was "not strange but natural." In time it came to seem natural to all of us that the Settlement should be there. If it is natural to feed the hungry and care for the sick, it is certainly natural to give pleasure to the young, comfort to the aged, and to minister to the deep-seated craving for social intercourse that all men feel. Whoever does it is rewarded by something which, if not

gratitude, is at least spontaneous and vital and lacks that irksome sense of obligation with which a substantial benefit is too often acknowledged.

In addition to the neighbors who responded to the receptions and classes, we found those who were too battered and oppressed to care for them. To these, however, was left that susceptibility to the bare offices of humanity which raises such offices into a bond of fellowship.

From the first it seemed understood that we were ready to perform the humblest neighborhood services. We were asked to wash the new-born babies, and to prepare the dead for burial, to nurse the sick, and to "mind the children."

Occasionally these neighborly offices unexpectedly uncovered ugly human traits. For six weeks after an operation we kept in one of our three bedrooms a forlorn little baby who, because he was born with a cleft palate,[6] was most unwelcome even to his mother, and we were horrified when he died of neglect a week after he was returned to his home; a little Italian bride of fifteen sought shelter with us one November evening, to escape her husband who had beaten her every night for a week when he returned home from work, because she had lost her wedding ring; two of us officiated quite alone at the birth of an illegitimate child because the doctor was late in arriving, and none of the honest Irish matrons would "touch the

---

4. **mitigate**: soften and make less severe.
5. **refutation**: disproof.
6. **cleft palate**: a lengthwise split in the roof of the mouth.

likes of her"; we ministered at the deathbed of a young man, who during a long illness of tuberculosis had received so many bottles of whiskey through the mistaken kindness of his friends, that the cumulative effect produced wild periods of exultation, in one of which he died.

We were also early impressed with the curious isolation of many of the immigrants; an Italian woman once expressed her pleasure in the red roses that she saw at one of our receptions in surprise that they had been "brought so fresh all the way from Italy." She would not believe for an instant that they had been grown in America. She said that she had lived in Chicago for six years and had never seen any roses, whereas in Italy she had seen them every summer in great profusion. During all that time, of course, the woman had lived within ten blocks of a florist's window; she had not been more than a five-cent car ride away from the public parks; but she had never dreamed of faring forth for herself, and no one had taken her. Her conception of America had been the untidy street in which she lived and had made her long struggle to adapt herself to American ways.

But in spite of some untoward experiences, we were constantly impressed with the uniform kindness and courtesy we received. Perhaps these first days laid the simple human foundations which are certainly essential for continuous living among the poor: first, genuine preference for residence in an industrial quarter to any other part of the city, because it is interesting and makes the human appeal; and second, the conviction, in the words of Canon Barnett, that the things which make men alike are finer and better than the things that keep them apart, and that these basic likenesses, if they are properly accentuated, easily transcend the less essential differences of race, language, creed and tradition.

Perhaps even in those first days we made a beginning toward that object which was afterwards stated in our charter: "To provide a center for a higher civic and social life; to institute and maintain educational and philanthropic[7] enterprises, and to investigate and improve the conditions in the industrial districts of Chicago."

---

7. **philanthropic:** charitable.

Unit 4: Poetry

Poetry is a way of taking life by the throat.
                                        Robert Frost

Poetry began ages ago as songs that expressed deeply felt emotion. These songs celebrated heroic people and important events, such as successful hunts or victorious battles. As language developed, the songs were written down. Because poetry is related to song, a good introduction is through music. Listen to the lyrics of your favorite song. How does it make you feel? How is it able to arouse those feelings?

Your answers may include comments about the song's words and their arrangement. You might also enjoy the rhythm or beat of the song. Through music, you'll discover that you are already familiar with some of the elements of poetry.

A poem can be about anything. Like the songs of ancient times, the first poem in this unit celebrates life. The speaker admires hard-working Americans, busy at their jobs. In another poem, two men repair a stone fence that separates their properties. The speaker in this poem wonders why people build such barriers. Different perspectives on friends are offered in two other poems.

Poets carefully choose and combine words to convey meaning as precisely as possible. You'll need to read each poem more than once to understand what is said, as well as to discover what is left unsaid. Your response to the poems in this unit will depend on the experiences and ideas you bring to each one. Just as with music, relax and enjoy poetry. Let its sound and meaning blend to create a special message just for you.

In what ways are ordinary people the backbone of a nation? In this poem written in the 1800s by Walt Whitman, the speaker hears the songs of everyday Americans as they celebrate their work and play. Read to decide if the poem still applies to people today.

THE JOLLY FLATBOATMEN (detail), 1848, George Caleb Bingham, Terra Museum of American Art, Daniel J. Terra Collection, Evanston, Illinois.

I Hear America Singing

Walt Whitman (1819–1892)

I hear America singing, the varied carols I hear,
Those of mechanics, each one singing his as it should be
    blithe[1] and strong,
The carpenter singing his as he measures his plank or beam,
The mason singing his as he makes ready for work, or leaves
    off work,
5 The boatman singing what belongs to him in his boat, the
    deckhand singing on the steamboat deck,
The shoemaker singing as he sits on his bench, the hatter
    singing as he stands,
The wood-cutter's song, the ploughboy's on his way in the
    morning, or at noon intermission or at sundown,
The delicious singing of the mother, or of the young wife at
    work, or of the girl sewing or washing,
Each singing what belongs to him or her and to none else,
10 The day what belongs to the day—at night the party of
    young fellows, robust, friendly,
Singing with open mouths their strong melodious songs.

---

1. **blithe:** cheerful.

Almost 100 years after Walt Whitman wrote "I Hear America Singing," Langston Hughes, a noted 20th century black writer, responded with this poem. Its speaker, too, sings a song of American life. But this poem is a reminder of the discrimination minorities have faced. Read to discover the speaker's message about the future.

I, Too, Sing America

Langston Hughes (1902–1967)

I, too, sing America.

I am the darker brother.
They send me to eat in the kitchen
When company comes,
5 But I laugh,
And eat well,
And grow strong.

Tomorrow,
I'll be at the table
10 When company comes.
Nobody'll dare
Say to me,
"Eat in the kitchen,"
Then.

15 Besides,
They'll see how beautiful I am
And be ashamed—

I, too, am America.

BLACK MANHATTAN, 1969, Romare Bearden, Collage on board, 25¼ x 21¼ inches. Photography: E. Lee White, Schomburg Center for Research in Black Culture, Art & Artifacts Division, The New York Public Library, Astor, Lenox and Tilden Foundations

*How well do you get along with your neighbor? In
"Mending Wall," the speaker and his neighbor meet
every spring to repair the stone wall that separates their
properties. Read to find out if both men agree that "Good
fences make good neighbors."*

Mending Wall

Robert Frost (1874–1963)

Something there is that doesn't love a wall,
That sends the frozen-ground-swell under it,
And spills the upper boulders in the sun;
And makes gaps even two can pass abreast.
5 The work of hunters is another thing:
I have come after them and made repair
Where they have left not one stone on a stone,
But they would have the rabbit out of hiding,
To please the yelping dogs. The gaps I mean,
10 No one has seen them made or heard them made,
But at spring mending-time we find them there.
I let my neighbor know beyond the hill;
And on a day we meet to walk the line
And set the wall between us once again.
15 We keep the wall between us as we go.
To each the boulders that have fallen to each.
And some are loaves and some so nearly balls
We have to use a spell to make them balance:
"Stay where you are until our backs are turned!"
20 We wear our fingers rough with handling them.
Oh, just another kind of outdoor game,
One on a side. It comes to little more:
There where it is we do not need the wall:
He is all pine and I am apple orchard.

25 My apple trees will never get across
And eat the cones under his pines, I tell him.
He only says, "Good fences make good neighbors."
Spring is the mischief in me, and I wonder
If I could put a notion in his head:

30 "*Why* do they make good neighbors? Isn't it
Where there are cows? But here there are no cows.
Before I built a wall I'd ask to know
What I was walling in or walling out,
And to whom I was like to give offense.

35 Something there is that doesn't love a wall,
That wants it down." I could say "Elves" to him,
But it's not elves exactly, and I'd rather
He said it for himself. I see him there
Bringing a stone grasped firmly by the top

40 In each hand, like an old-stone savage armed.
He moves in darkness as it seems to me,
Not of woods only and the shade of trees.
He will not go behind his father's saying,
And he likes having thought of it so well

45 He says again, "Good fences make good neighbors."

What do friends mean to you? Read to find out how much the speaker reveals about a friendship in this poem of just six lines.

Poem

Langston Hughes (1902–1967)

I loved my friend.
He went away from me.
There's nothing more to say.
The poem ends.
5   Soft as it began—
I loved my friend.

*How do you feel when you are by yourself? The speaker
in this poem considers thoughts to be best friends. Read
to decide if you agree.*

Thoughts

Sara Teasdale (1884–1933)

When I am all alone
    Envy me most,
Then my thoughts flutter round me
    In a glimmering host;

5 Some dressed in silver,
    Some dressed in white,
Each like a taper
    Blossoming light;

Most of them merry,
10   Some of them grave,
Each of them lithe
    As willows that wave;

Some bearing violets,
    Some bearing bay,
15 One with a burning rose
    Hidden away—

When I am all alone
    Envy me then,
For I have better friends
20   Than women and men.

Do you think society encourages people to be independent thinkers or to be conformists? Conformists are people who follow the customs, fashions, tastes, and ideas of others. The speaker in this poem describes a man who fit in with society but died leaving no personal influence on it. Read to discover if the title of this poem accurately describes this man.

The Unknown Citizen

W. H. Auden (1907–1973)

(To JS/07/M/378   This Marble Monument Is Erected by the State)

He was found by the Bureau of Statistics to be
One against whom there was no official complaint,
And all the reports on his conduct agree
That, in the modern sense of an old-fashioned word, he
    was a saint,
5 For in everything he did he served the Greater Community.
Except for the War till the day he retired
He worked in a factory and never got fired,
But satisfied his employers, Fudge Motors Inc.
Yet he wasn't a scab[1] or odd in his views,
10 For his Union reports that he paid his dues,
(Our report on his Union shows it was sound)
And our Social Psychology workers found
That he was popular with his mates and liked a drink.
The Press are convinced that he bought a paper every day
And that his reactions to advertisements were normal in
15   every way.
Policies taken out in his name prove that he was fully insured,
And his Health-card shows he was once in hospital but left
    it cured.

---

1. scab: person who takes the job of a worker who is on strike.

UNTITLED (CROWD), 1958, David Park, courtesy of Mr. Harry Cohn, Hillsborough, California, photograph: John Berggruen Gallery, San Francisco, California

Both Producers Research and High-Grade Living declare
He was fully sensible to the advantages of the Installment Plan
20 And had everything necessary to the Modern Man,
A phonograph, a radio, a car and a frigidaire.
Our researchers into Public Opinion are content
That he held the proper opinions for the time of year;
When there was peace, he was for peace; when there was
    war, he went.
25 He was married and added five children to the population,
Which our Eugenist[2] says was the right number for a parent of
    his generation,
And our teachers report that he never interfered with
    their education.
Was he free? Was he happy? The question is absurd:
Had anything been wrong, we should certainly have heard.

---

2. **Eugenist:** scientist who deals with improving the human race by controlling factors influencing heredity.

Why might someone be glad to be a "nobody"? Emily Dickinson, who wrote this poem, preferred a quiet life. She rarely left her home, where she wrote thousands of poems that went unpublished until after her death. Emily Dickinson never knew that she would become one of America's best-known poets. Read to decide if this recognition would have pleased her.

I'm Nobody! Who are you?

Emily Dickinson (1830–1886)

I'm Nobody! Who are you?
Are you—Nobody—Too?
Then there's a pair of us!
Don't tell! they'd advertise—you know!

5   How dreary—to be—Somebody!
How public—like a Frog—
To tell one's name—the livelong June—
To an admiring Bog!

Unit 5: Drama

*A play should give you something to
think about. When I see a play and understand
it the first time, then I know it can't be much good.*

T.S. Eliot

A drama or play is unlike any other literature in this anthology. Plays are written to be performed in front of an audience. Because plays are meant to be seen as well as heard, you face an exciting challenge as a reader. Your imagination must be active as you pretend to take a seat in the audience, watching the action onstage.

Be assured that the playwright assists you in visualizing the setting, characters, and action of the play. In the script, or written text of the play, stage directions explain how characters deliver their dialogue, or words. Stage directions also detail the scenery, lighting, and sound effects needed to create the setting, or time and place.

Because drama is such a different type of literature, you may want to read the following excerpts in this unit by yourself first. Get to know the characters and the roles they play in the action or plot. Picture the setting. Think about the theme or message communicated by the playwright. After you become familiar with the plays, you may be eager to move from your seat in the audience to center stage, acting out these excerpts with your classmates.

Do you know someone who never fulfilled his dreams? Willy Loman, the main character in this play, is such a person. Willy is a traveling salesman in his 60s. Throughout the play, he recalls scenes from his past that appear on stage.

In the excerpt below, Willy has returned home from a business trip exhausted and discouraged. He is reliving an event from the high school days of his sons, Biff and Happy. Willy's wife Linda and his sons' friend Bernard also appear in this scene from the Loman family's past. Read to find clues that may explain why Willy never fulfilled his dreams.

From
Death of a Salesman

Arthur Miller (1915–   )

Willy: Just wanna be careful with those girls, Biff, that's all. Don't make any promises. No promises of any kind. Because a girl, y'know, they always believe what you tell 'em, and you're very young, Biff, you're too young to be talking seriously to girls. *(Light rises on the kitchen. Willy, talking, shuts the refrigerator door and comes downstage to the kitchen table. He pours milk into a glass. He is totally immersed in himself, smiling faintly.)* **Willy:** Too young entirely, Biff. You want to watch your schooling first. Then when you're all set, there'll be plenty of girls for a boy like you. *(He smiles broadly at a kitchen chair.)* That so? The girls pay for you? *(He laughs.)* Boy, you must really be makin' a hit. *(Willy is gradually addressing— physically—a point offstage, speaking through the wall of the kitchen, and his voice has been rising in volume to that of a normal conversation.)* **Willy:** I been wondering why you polish the car so careful. Ha! Don't leave the hubcaps, boys. Get the chamois to the hubcaps. Happy, use newspaper on the windows, it's the easiest thing. Show him how to do it, Biff! You see, Happy? Pad it up, use it like a pad. That's it, that's it, good work. You're doin' all right, Hap. *(He pauses, then nods in approbation for a few seconds, then looks upward.)* Biff, first thing we gotta do when we get time is clip that big branch over the house. Afraid it's gonna fall in a storm and hit the roof. Tell you what. We get a rope and sling her around, and then we climb up there with a couple of saws and take her down. Soon as you finish the car, boys, I wanna see ya. I got a surprise for you, boys.

Biff: *(Offstage)* Whatta ya got, Dad?

Willy: No, you finish first. Never leave a job till you're finished—remember that. *(Looking toward the "big trees")* Biff, up in Albany I saw a beautiful hammock. I think I'll buy it next trip, and we'll hang it right between those two elms. Wouldn't that be something? Just swingin' there under those branches. Boy that would be...

(Young Biff and Young Happy appear from the direction Willy was addressing. Happy carries rags and a pail of water. Biff, wearing a sweater with a block "S," carries a football.)

Biff: *(Pointing in the direction of the car offstage)* How's that, Pop, professional?

Willy: Terrific. Terrific job, boys. Good work, Biff.

Happy: Where's the surprise, Pop?

Willy: In the back seat of the car.

Happy: Boy! *(He runs off.)*

Biff: What is it, Dad? Tell me, what'd you buy?

Willy: *(Laughing, cuffs him)* Never mind, something I want you to have.

Biff: *(Turns and starts off)* What is it, Hap?

Happy: *(Offstage)* It's a punching bag!

Biff: Oh, Pop!

Willy: It's got Gene Tunney's signature on it!

(Happy runs onstage with a punching bag.)

Biff: Gee, how'd you know we wanted a punching bag?

Willy: Well, it's the finest thing for the timing.

Happy: *(Lies down on his back and pedals with his feet)* I'm losing weight, you notice, Pop?

Willy: *(To Happy)* Jumping rope is good too.

Biff: Did you see the new football I got?

Willy: *(Examining the ball)* Where'd you get a new ball?

Biff: The coach told me to practice my passing.

Willy: That so? And he gave you the ball, heh?

Biff: Well, I borrowed it from the locker room. *(He laughs confidentially.)*

Willy: *(Laughing with him at the theft)* I want you to return that.

Happy: I told you he wouldn't like it!

Biff: *(Angrily)* Well, I'm bringing it back!

Willy: *(Stopping the incipient argument, to Happy)* Sure, he's gotta practice with a regulation ball, doesn't he? *(To Biff)* Coach'll probably congratulate you on your initiative!

Biff: Oh, he keeps congratulating my initiative all the time, Pop.

Willy: That's because he likes you. If somebody else took that ball there'd be an uproar. So what's the report, boys, what's the report?

Biff: Where'd you go this time, Dad? Gee we were lonesome for you.

Willy: (*Pleased, puts an arm around each boy and they come down to the apron*) Lonesome, heh?

Biff: Missed you every minute.

Willy: Don't say? Tell you a secret, boys. Don't breathe it to a soul. Someday I'll have my own business, and I'll never have to leave home any more.

Happy: Like Uncle Charley, heh?

Willy: Bigger than Uncle Charley! Because Charley is not—liked. He's liked, but he's not—well liked.

Biff: Where'd you go this time, Dad?

Willy: Well, I got on the road, and I went north to Providence. Met the Mayor.

Biff: The Mayor of Providence!

Willy: He was sitting in the hotel lobby.

Biff: What'd he say?

Willy: He said, "Morning!" And I said, "You got a fine city here, Mayor." And then he had coffee with me. And then I went to Waterbury. Waterbury is a fine city. Big clock city, the famous Waterbury clock. Sold a nice bill there. And then Boston—Boston is the cradle of the Revolution. A fine city. And a couple of other towns in Mass., and on to Portland and Bangor and straight home!

Biff: Gee, I'd love to go with you sometime, Dad.

Willy: Soon as summer comes.

Happy: Promise?

Willy: You and Hap and I, and I'll show you all the towns. America is full of beautiful towns and fine, upstanding people. And they know me, boys, they know me up and down New England. The finest people. And when I bring you fellas up, there'll be open sesame for all of us, 'cause one thing, boys: I have friends. I can park my car in any street in New England, and the cops protect it like their own. This summer, heh?

Biff and Happy: (*Together*) Yeah! You bet!

Willy: We'll take our bathing suits.

Happy: We'll carry your bags, Pop!

Willy: Oh, won't that be something! Me comin' into the Boston stores with you boys carryin' my bags. What a sensation!

(*Biff is prancing around, practicing passing the ball.*)

Willy: You nervous, Biff, about the game?

Biff: Not if you're gonna be there.

Willy: What do they say about you in school, now that they made you captain?

Happy: There's a crowd of girls behind him everytime the classes change.

Biff: (*Taking Willy's hand*) This Saturday, Pop, this Saturday—just for you, I'm going to break through for a touchdown.

Happy: You're supposed to pass.

Biff: I'm takin' one play for Pop. You watch me, Pop, and when I take off my helmet, that means I'm breakin' out. you watch me crash through that line!

Willy: (*Kisses Biff*) Oh, wait'll I tell this in Boston!

(*Bernard enters in knickers. He is younger than Biff, earnest and loyal, a worried boy.*)

Bernard: Biff, where are you? You're supposed to study with me today.

From left to right: Bernard, Happy, Linda, Willy Loman, and Biff.

Willy: Hey, looka Bernard. What're you lookin' so anemic[1] about, Bernard?

Bernard: He's gotta study, Uncle Willy. He's got Regents next week.

Happy: *(Tauntingly, spinning Bernard around)* Let's box, Bernard!

Bernard: Biff! *(He gets away from Happy.)* Listen, Biff, I heard Mr. Birnbaum say that if you don't start studyin' math he's gonna flunk you, and you won't graduate. I heard him!

Willy: You better study with him, Biff. Go ahead now.

Bernard: I heard him!

Biff: Oh Pop, you didn't see my sneakers! *(He holds up a foot for Willy to look at.)*

Willy: Hey, that's a beautiful job of printing!

Bernard: *(Wiping his glasses)* Just because he printed University of Virginia on his sneakers doesn't mean they've got to graduate him, Uncle Willy!

Willy: *(Angrily)* What're you talking about? With scholarships to three universities they're gonna flunk him?

Bernard: But I heard Mr. Birnbaum say—

Willy: Don't be a pest, Bernard! *(To his boys)* What an anemic!

Bernard: Okay, I'm waiting for you in my house, Biff.

(Bernard goes off. The Lomans laugh.)

Willy: Bernard is not well liked, is he?

Biff: He's liked, but he's not well liked.

Happy: That's right, Pop.

Willy: That's just what I mean. Bernard can get the best marks in school, y'understand, but when he gets out in the business world, y'understand, you are going to be five times

---

1. anemic: pale in appearance.

ahead of him. That's why I thank Almighty God you're both built like Adonises.[2] Because the man who makes an appearance in the business world, the man who creates personal interest, is the man who gets ahead. Be liked and you will never want. You take me, for instance. I never have to wait in line to see a buyer. "Willy Loman is here!" That's all they have to know, and I go right through.

Biff: Did you knock them dead, Pop?

Willy: Knocked 'em cold in Providence, slaughtered 'em in Boston.

Happy: *(On his back, pedaling again)* I'm losing weight, you notice, Pop?

(Linda enters, as of old, a ribbon in her hair, carrying a basket of washing.)

Linda: *(With youthful energy)* Hello, dear!

Willy: Sweetheart!

Linda: How'd the Chevvy run?

Willy: Chevrolet, Linda, is the greatest car ever built. *(To the boys)* Since when do you let your mother carry wash up the stairs?

Biff: Grab hold there, boy!

Happy: Where to, Mom?

Linda: Hang them up on the line. And you better go down to your friends, Biff. The cellar is full of boys. They don't know what to do with themselves.

Biff: Ah, when Pop comes home they can wait!

Willy: *(Laughs appreciatively)* You better go down and tell them what to do, Biff.

Biff: I think I'll have them sweep out the furnace room.

Willy: Good work, Biff.

Biff: *(Goes through wall-line of kitchen to doorway at back and calls down)* Fellas! Everybody sweep out the furnace room! I'll be right down!

Voices: All right! Okay, Biff.

Biff: George and Sam and Frank, come out back! We're hangin' up the wash! Come on, Hap, on the double!

(He and Happy carry out the basket.)

Linda: The way they obey him!

Willy: Well, that's training, the training. I'm tellin' you, I was sellin' thousands and thousands, but I had to come home.

Linda: Oh, the whole block'll be at that game. Did you sell anything?

Willy: I did five hundred gross in Providence and seven hundred gross in Boston.

Linda: No! Wait a minute, I've got a pencil. *(She pulls pencil and paper out of her apron pocket.)* That makes your commission...Two hundred—my God! Two hundred and twelve dollars!

Willy: Well, I didn't figure it yet, but...

Linda: How much did you do?

Willy: Well, I—I did—about a hundred and eighty gross in Providence. Well, no,—it came to—roughly two hundred gross on the whole trip.

Linda: *(Without hesitation)* Two hundred gross. That's... *(She figures.)*

Willy: The trouble was that three of the stores were half closed for inventory in Boston. Otherwise I woulda broke records.

Linda: Well, it makes seventy dollars and some pennies. That's very good.

---

2. **Adonises:** very handsome men; in Greek mythology, Adonis was a handsome hunter.

Linda and Willy Loman

Willy: What do we owe?

Linda: Well, on the first there's sixteen dollars on the refrigerator—

Willy: Why sixteen?

Linda: Well, the fan broke, so it was a dollar eighty.

Willy: But it's brand new.

Linda: Well, the man said that's the way it is. Till they work themselves in, y'know.

(They move through the wall-line into the kitchen.)

Willy: I hope we didn't get stuck on that machine.

Linda: They got the biggest ads of any of them!

Willy: I know, it's a fine machine. What else?

Linda: Well, there's nine-sixty for the washing machine. And for the vacuum cleaner there's three and a half due on the fifteenth. Then the roof, you got twenty-one dollars remaining.

Willy: It don't leak, does it?

Linda: No, they did a wonderful job. Then you owe Frank for the carburetor.

Willy: I'm not going to pay that man! That goddam Chevrolet, they ought to prohibit the manufacture of that car!

Linda: Well, you owe him three and a half. And odds and ends, comes to around a hundred and twenty dollars by the fifteenth.

Willy: A hundred and twenty dollars! My God, if business doesn't pick up I don't know what I'm gonna do!

Linda: Well, next week you'll do better.

Willy: Oh, I'll knock 'em dead next week. I'll go to Hartford. I'm very well liked in Hartford. You know, the trouble is, Linda, people don't seem to take to me.

(They move onto the forestage.)

Linda: Oh, don't be foolish.

Death of a Salesman   **91**

Willy: I know it when I walk in. They seem to laugh at me.

Linda: Why? Why would they laugh at you? Don't talk that way, Willy. *(Willy moves to the edge of the stage. Linda goes into the kitchen and starts to darn stockings.)*

Willy: I don't know the reason for it, but they just pass me by. I'm not noticed.

Linda: But you're doing wonderful, dear. You're making seventy to a hundred dollars a week.

Willy: But I gotta be at it ten, twelve hours a day. Other men—I don't know—they do it easier. I don't know why—I can't stop myself—I talk too much. A man oughta come in with a few words. One thing about Charley. He's a man of few words, and they respect him.

Linda: You don't talk too much, you're just lively.

Willy: *(Smiling)* Well, I figure, what the hell, life is short, a couple of jokes. *(To himself)* I joke too much! *(The smile goes.)*

Linda: Why? You're—

Willy: I'm fat. I'm very—foolish to look at, Linda. I didn't tell you, but Christmas time I happened to be calling on F. H. Stewarts, and a salesman I know, as I was going in to see the buyer I heard him say some-

Linda and Willy Loman

Inge Morath, Magnum Photos

thing about—walrus. And I—I cracked him right across the face. I won't take that. I simply will not take that. But they do laugh at me. I know that.

Linda: Darling...

Willy: I gotta overcome it. I know I gotta overcome it. I'm not dressing to advantage, maybe.

Linda: Willy, darling, you're the handsomest man in the world—

Willy: Oh, no, Linda.

Linda: To me you are. *(Slight pause)* The handsomest.

Have you ever faced an obstacle that seemed impossible to overcome? In 1921 Franklin D. Roosevelt took ill at his summer home at Campobello, New Brunswick, Canada. Although stricken with polio, Roosevelt was determined to remain active in politics.

This excerpt from the play takes place two years later. Roosevelt and his mother Sara argue in the living room of the family home in New York City. Sara thinks her son's wife Eleanor and his friend Louie Howe push him too hard. She urges her son to forget running for public office. Roosevelt refuses to give up. Read to discover the strength one man finds to overcome an obstacle.

From

Sunrise at Campobello

Dore Schary (1905–1980)

Sara: Of course, dear. *(Eleanor leaves. Sara sips her tea, thinking of the opening gambit. She finds one.)* Oh, Franklin, I'm getting some men at Hyde Park[1] to determine how we can electrify the lift. It is, after all, only a large-size dumbwaiter[2] and I—

FDR: *(Quickly)* No! *(Perhaps he's been too sharp.)* I mean, please don't. The exercise of pulling those ropes is helpful to me. I need it for my arms and shoulders. So, if you're thinking of me— please don't change the dumbwaiter.

Sara: I feel you're doing too much, physically.

FDR: I wish I could do more. Mama— it's only my legs that are temporarily bothered. The rest of me is as healthy as ever.

Sara: I know that. I know that. I talk to the doctors. They tell me. But sometimes I think that Eleanor, certainly only with motives of deep love, and that ugly little man, push you too rapidly.

FDR: I don't think so. Dr. Draper doesn't think so. And please, Mama, don't refer to Louie Howe any longer with that unpleasant phrase. I've endured it too long as it is.

Sara: *(Walking about, genuinely disturbed)* Franklin, your tone of voice is very disturbing to me.

FDR: Mama, if possible, I should like to have a quiet talk with you. I should like not to quarrel. Now, Mama, I

---

1. **Hyde Park:** the Roosevelt estate in Hyde Park, New York.
2. **dumbwaiter:** a small elevator.

know how upset you've been. This is a real wrench for you. But I'm going to get over this—and—if I don't—a big *if*—I shall have to become accustomed to braces and canes and wheel chairs. And so will you.

Sara: Oh, Franklin—

FDR: Please, let me finish. Louie Howe—*(Sara makes an involuntary grimace.)* Ma*ma*, stop that. Louie Howe told me, while I was in the hospital after Campobello, that I had one of two choices. I could lie on my back, be a country squire and write books—*or*—get up and become President of the United States. *Now*—I believe Louie's dreams are far too bright—but I've no intention of retiring to Hyde Park and rusticating.[3]

Sara: *(Quietly)* Franklin, when you were a little boy, your dear father took you for a visit to the White House to see President Cleveland.

FDR: *(Fidgets)* Ma*ma*, I know.

Sara: *(Firmly)* Let me finish. And President Cleveland said, "I make a strange wish for you. It is that you may never be President of the United States."

FDR: Well, he was playing the odds in wishing that.

Sara: Your Cousin Teddy died because of ambitious people around him. Died because he didn't know when to stop—didn't know that you can't make it the same world for all people.

FDR: Maybe we can't. But it seems to me that every human has an obligation in his own way to make some little stab at trying.

Sara: It's not such a bad world, Franklin—not at all.

Franklin D. Roosevelt with his mother Sara (left) and his wife Eleanor in 1929.

AP/Wide World Photos

FDR: I have no personal complaints. I'm lucky. I had rich parents.

Sara: Don't be self-conscious about that Franklin. Advantages of birth should be worn like clothes, with grace and comfort.

FDR: *(A familiar tale—and he knows it.)* Yes—yes. *Noblesse oblige.*[4] The poor will always be with us. We went through that when I sold the mining stock.

Sara: On reflection—you must admit that was a childish gesture.

FDR: *(The heat is on.)* I would not hang onto stock bringing me an income over the tortured bodies of miners who lived as though they were in the middle ages. These are different times. The attitude of *noblesse oblige* is archaic.[5]

---

3. **rusticating:** living in the country.
4. **noblesse oblige:** the obligation of the upper class to behave in a certain manner.
5. **archaic:** old-fashioned.

Sara: Franklin!

FDR: It's another name for indifference.

Sara: How dare you! You are talking to your mother. Even if I were to agree with your romantic political ideas, it would be absurd for you to consider running for public office. The traveling and the speeches would be an enormous strain for you.

FDR: At the moment I'm not running for anything—and I won't until I can get around and stand up on my own two feet—but that doesn't mean I have to go into hiding.

Sara: *(Icily)* I'm not asking you to do that. I'm asking you to be sensible—to take up a permanent residence in Hyde Park where you could be comfortable—where you could use the time for resting and regain your strength.

FDR: I love Hyde Park. But I want to use it—not let it bury me.

Sara: That's a terrible thing to say.

FDR: You know what I mean.

Sara: No, Franklin, I do not know what you mean. I only know that your stubbornness is not only your strength but your weakness. And you needn't—

FDR: *(Getting angry)* I needn't do a damn thing! I am not going to let myself go down a drain. A bad beating either breaks the stick or the student—Well, I'm not broken. I'm not settling for the life of an ailing invalid. And I will no longer abide implications, innuendos or insinuations that I do so.

Sara: I don't want you getting angry. It's not good for you.

FDR: *(Heatedly)* It's damn good. For me.

Sara: Franklin, I wonder if you truly know what is good for you. You come by your Dutch stubbornness by birth. And, Franklin, some of that Dutch stubbornness is mine—from long association. *(She now becomes firm and dominant.)* Franklin, many many years ago, when I was a little girl, I sailed to China with my father on a clipper ship. As we rounded Cape Horn, we headed into a fearful storm. My father, eager and headstrong, urged the Captain to head into the sea—to fight through the storm. But fortunately the Captain of the ship was a better sailor than my father. He wanted to save his ship. He trimmed sails, gave orders to "heave to," rode out the storm safely, and then, when the heavy weather was gone, we were able to sail ahead and nothing was lost—nothing. Be wise, Franklin—ride out the storm. *(A pause. Sara, emotionally wrought-up by now, strikes hotter.)* Son, let me ask, you—what do you believe I want for you—obscurity? Invalidism? Do you believe that this is my ambition for you? Having been a mother for over forty years, do you think this is what I want? Any dream you ever had or could have, I have. All pain you have felt, I have felt. *(By now she is sharp and hard.)* I don't want to see you hurt.

FDR: That's enough. There'll be no more talking—no more. *(Sara goes to the side of the room. She is moved and hurt, but genuinely trying to cover her emotions. FDR has discarded his pipe and is trying to cover what he feels. At this moment, Eleanor enters. She sees at a glance that there is tension in the* room. *Sara turns her back a moment, then faces Eleanor, contained but cold.)*

Sara: Eleanor, I cannot have dinner with you tonight.

Eleanor: Ma*ma*—you may have quarreled with Franklin—but not with the rest of the family. *(Sara is mum.)* Please?

Sara: *(Reluctantly)* Very well—I'll join you. Excuse me. *(Eleanor nods. Sara looks at FDR. He by now is depressed rather than angry. Sara leaves. Eleanor watches FDR, who sits glumly in his chair for a moment, then whirls around to her.)*

Eleanor: Franklin, anything needed?

FDR: Nothing. *(Eleanor hesitates a moment, then exits. FDR sits for a moment. He is low and dispirited. Suddenly he looks up and toward the crutches. He is in his mind challenging his mother and what she has implied. He decides to prove something to himself and to her. He quickly rolls his chair to the crutches. He places them on his knees and then moves to a clearer section of the room. He puts up one crutch, and then the other, attempting to rise off the chair by himself and onto the crutches. He is confident and determined. He is half out of the chair when the crutch slips away from him and he crumples to the floor. He lies there a moment, a look of sickening defeat and humiliation and pain on his face. He rubs his leg. Then alarmed that perhaps he has been heard, he attempts to get back into his chair. This is not an easy task, but slowly, carefully and painfully, he manages—again almost meeting disaster, but finally overcoming his obstacles, he makes the security and safety of his chair. He pauses, exhausted and in pain. Then he reaches for his crutches, rolls the chair to each crutch successively, and finally by stretching and bending, gets them into his hands and over his knees. He sits now, his head bent forward, a portrait of a man who has lost a battle that seemed so very important. Slowly he leans back, his face now hard and grim, but determined. Then, stubbornly, he places the crutches before him and prepares to try again to rise from the chair. He begins his efforts, but we do not know if he succeeds or not, as*

The Curtain Falls